The REAL-DEAL Bridal Bible

THE ULTIMATE WEDDING PLANNER
TO HELP YOU BLUSH LIKE A BRIDE
AND PLAN LIKE A BITCH

ALESSANDRA MACALUSO

Table 1
The Calm
Before the Storm

The

Table 3
The Bridal
Party

Table 5
Haters

Table 7
Reception Hall

Dance

Table 9
Vendors

Table 11
Etiquette, & the
Etiquette-less

Table 13
Here Comes
the Groom

Table 15
Hair, Makeup,
& Your Inner
Fashionista

Table 17
Your "To Do"
Lists

Table 19
Useful Tips

Dais

Table 2
Pre-Planning
Checklist

Table 4
In-laws & Other
Family Members

Table 6
Ceremony

Table 8
The Dress

Floor

Table 10
Bridal
Showers & Big
Box Marts

Table 12
Your Mental
Health

Table 14
Bling Bling
Miss Thing

Table 16
Honeymoon

Table 18
Communication

Table 20
The
After Party

Dedication and Thank You

This book is dedicated to every bride-to-be, particularly those who want a stress-free wedding, and to every person who may one day get married. It's also dedicated to those who have already been down the aisle, because they especially will nod in agreement and laugh their asses off reliving the shenanigans.

If you've been given this book as a gift, please know that you are not a 'bitch' in the derogatory sense of the word. The person who gifted this to you thinks you are a 'smart bitch', a 'savvy bitch', a 'bad-ass bridal bitch with a sense of humor'. In other words, it's a bitchin' compliment to you that you've received this book.

Thank you to my family, friends, and others who have supported me through this writing process and shared their stories for this book. To my parents, for setting a wonderful example for me to follow in my own married life. And to my husband, the poor but patient soul who didn't realize what he signed up for when he married a writer, but who sticks around, anyway. I love you, and thank you.

Table of Contents

The Real-Deal Bridal Bible

The Must-Have Guide for Wedding Planning, and Life Beyond

Something mystical can happen when you take a perfectly sane woman and place a diamond ring on her finger. Doctors have attempted to describe the phenomenon for years. There seems to be a chemical reaction between the compounds that make up the ring and the molecules in the skin and, upon contact, they have been known to create the virus: cRzybTch1.

We've all encountered cRzybTch1 at some point in our lives. Even if we haven't contracted it ourselves, we've all known someone close to us who was infected with this unfortunate and highly aggressive virus.

Curiously, it has been found that cRzybTch1 can skip entirely over the person wearing the ring and somehow infect those around her, creating a hybrid strain: jElousbTch2. Doctors are not certain as to how jElousbTch2 transpires, because the strain keeps morphing every time they come close to controlling it.

Even more alarming, it has been known to continue to transfer hosts and morph into other viruses, such as pSychoMIL3, CRzySIL4 and the rapidly-spreading THeythinkiTstheirWddnG5, 6 and 7. Some symptoms include: uninvited opinion-giving, passive-aggressive comments followed by scary, wide-eyed smiles, and a majorly bitchy attitude on your big day (a hybrid of jElousbTch2, also known as iTsnotaBoutMesoiLLsitHereandpout).

These viruses are so powerful that entire companies have been known to be infected, the victims of a new strain: leTsmiLkthemdRy9. Symptoms of leTsmiLkthemdRy9 include: pushing upon couples frivolous items disguised as "necessities," the ability to stealthily drain bank accounts, and some seriously hardcore marketing.

Yes, these are very threatening and highly intellectual viruses and, sadly, these strains can travel back and somehow affect the once clear-headed, sanity-filled bride-to-be.

But there is hope. You can protect yourself and those you love from cRzybTch1 and the rest of these viruses. You're holding the only known vaccine: *"The Real-Deal Bridal Bible."* Some side effects may include: increase in sanity, decrease in bullshit, ability to refrain from launching in-laws off the nearest bridge, fattening of the wallet, clarity of the mind, increase in sex drive, and bigger boobs. (Alright, maybe not that last one.)

There's no need to ask your doctor if *"The Real-Deal Bridal Bible"* is right for you, as time and units are limited. Just be sure to vaccinate yourself and your loved ones right away.

Who's This Book For?

This book is for brides-to-be, who are traditional at heart, but who still want to keep their edge. It's for the bride who is interested in letting her individuality shine through while still making Grandma happy. For those special ladies who possess the ability to see – and laugh at – the truth of this crazy time, and for those who want to be armed with information and resources to prepare them for what's really about to go down.

"*The Real-Deal Bridal Bible*" will serve as a guide to keep you grounded and sane while planning your big day. This book will not advise you on the trendiest cakes or hottest bridesmaid dresses, and it doesn't come with your traditional bridal bells and whistles. It's a real-deal, raw guide for brides about the important things you will encounter during your wedding planning, as well as *after* you say "I do." It's about navigating through this crazy time, finding your own way, and getting married on your own terms – while keeping your sanity, finances, and relationships intact.

Quite frankly, I don't give a shiny tiara about your place settings or the date you chose. Congratulations and good for you - but that's not why I'm here. I'm here to shed light upon the ugly in planning your nuptials. I'm here to talk about the down and dirty, roll-your-sleeves-up, crazy cocktail hour shenanigans that go on that you need to know about. I'm here to prepare you for the freak show that those closest to you will put on during your planning; to teach you how to coolly raise your glass, swig your mimosa, and point your finger and laugh at the hot mess that bridal blasphemy has brought out in everyone around you as you stay calm in your comfy cozy seat in Sanesville. Because people. Will. Go. In. Sane. I don't care if your family is the direct descendants of June fucking Cleaver – there will be shenanigans. So, pull up a chair – you're seated right next to me.

This book is also for bridesmaids, mothers, in-laws, and groomsmen. It is for shower planners and anyone else involved in someone's wedding planning process, so they may better understand the obstacles today's bride will encounter while coordinating her big day. It is for husbands-to-be, to serve as a guide to understanding and dealing with your bride and adjusting to your future together once the wedding has passed. It's also a guide for post-brides who are settling into their new lives and embarking on this exciting journey of marriage.

This book is armed with great resources, things you need to know, and helpful ways to deal with all of the stressors – both expected and unexpected – that arise during this special and crazy time. It will guide you, prepare you, and keep you in check and on track with what's important during your occasional bouts of "bridal brain." Think of it as a dear friend that will offer you sound advice, along with an occasional bitch-slap of reality to help you stay the course.

So, what's the reality?

When people hear the word "wedding," especially those close to you, everyone gushes. Suddenly it's all about the dress, the cake, the shower, the reception hall. Rarely is it about the marriage – the actual reason you are throwing a wedding in the first place.

Sure, you will occasionally get the old "marriage is work" speech from a parent or friend, but this is often pooh-poohed or dismissed. And besides, rarely at this point in your walkin'-on-the-clouds frame of mind are you going to stop and listen or heed any advice. Why would you? You are too busy searching for a dress, choosing a bridal party, tasting cakes, and partaking in a slew of other things that you certainly "must do" at this point in your life.

Meanwhile, the tiny little snowball is chugging along, on its way to a full-blown avalanche. This is all good and fine. Everyone loves a fluffy white snowball. That is, until it gains speed, multiplies in size, and takes you out completely.

Suddenly, it seems okay to put off responsibility and dip into savings accounts during the one time in our lives we should, ironically, be doing just the opposite. It's acceptable to let people into our lives, knowingly or unknowingly, who will tell us what to do and how to spend our money to ensure us a "happy ever after." It's fun, right?

Know what's not fun? Hair loss. Fits of rage. Finding your punk ass locked in a closet hiding from everyone you know while guzzling wine straight from a box, wondering what god forsaken mess you've brought upon yourself by making the seemingly simple decision to marry your best friend. It's very easy to deplete our funds and stress ourselves out during a time that should be wonderful.

And who could blame us? Society encourages the chaos, and no one prepares us for it. This generation of brides is like a social science experiment that has gone horribly wrong, and the result is a giant Frankenstein in a big white ball gown with bling'd-out bolts in its neck.

Our experience planning a wedding is a far cry from what our parents experienced. It's a different world now. Sadly, consumerism has dug in and held tight to what should be the most intimate, most special event of our lives, and has spit out an overwhelming list of expectations that are sure to create a bridezilla out of anyone.

It's time to slam on the brakes.

Who am I?

My name is Alessandra, and I am a recovering bride. I've been clean for about six years now.

Through my own planning of a three-hundred-person wedding, and the insane amount and different types of weddings I have attended over the past few years, I certainly have experienced all types of bridal bashes and blunders. Katherine Heigl's "Jane" in the movie *27 Dresses* ain't got nothin' on me. I want to share those experiences with you so you learn from them.

I don't tout myself as some relationship guru, or someone who did everything right in terms of my own wedding planning. Much of what I bring to you in this book comes out of my own mistakes and experiences, and I share them openly here.

I researched a great deal for this book and interviewed several people who have planned their wedding or someone else's, or who are in the industry themselves. I even interviewed therapists, because you know, *free therapy*, but also because they have great perspective as to what we can do to keep our marriage healthy after our vows have been exchanged. Because of their real, raw advice and willingness to share their experiences with me, I am able to present this book to you.

I wrote this book, also, to learn from those who have been in successful and unsuccessful marriages who were kind enough to tell their stories. I wanted to see how people who come from all sorts of families with different dynamics, expectations and situations learned to navigate through these relationships and find what works for them. Some instances were hysterically funny, others were painfully sad, but all of them were real, and we can take something from each of them.

I plan to keep this book on my own bookshelf as a real and useful reference for when the going gets tough, or for a good laugh, in good times and bad. I hope you will, too.

Navigation

As you can see, I have structured the table of contents of this book in the form of a reception hall seating chart (or "Reading Chart," if you will). The "tables" serve as chapters, representing people and situations you may encounter during your wedding planning.

Every bride is different, as are her traditions, so you may not experience all of these the same. But unless you are planning a wedding in Swahili and have no family on your side or your future spouse's, chances are you'll come across most of these instances. My goal is to help you prepare for them and to make sure you are happy, healthy, and have everything in perspective for your big day. Hopefully the tools and advice I offer in this book will even help you throughout your marriage as well. Visit each "table" in this book, just as you would visit each table at your wedding reception, you gracious bride, you.

Every so often throughout the book we will make our way back to the Dais, where you and your hubby will sit, just as you should do on your wedding day and throughout your married life. Drop in and spend some time with all the "tables," and be sure to mingle and say hello. But always remember to go back to the Dais, the place where it's just the two of you.

So, no matter if you are planning a wedding, planning to get out of planning a wedding, planning on planning a traditional wedding, planning to never plan another wedding, or just plain tired of the damn planning process, I'm glad we are all here. Throw on your silly bachelorette penis hat, have a seat, dim the lights, light a candle, and pour yourself a glass of wine. I'd like to propose to you some entertainment. I hope you enjoy my book.

Table #1:
The Calm before
the Storm

The day my now-husband Greg proposed to me is crystal-clear in my mind. Although it was meant to be a surprise, I knew it was coming. My dad, an off-the-boat Italian who can't hide his emotions no matter how hard he tries, totally gave it away.

I had been dating Greg for three years at that point. We had gone away a few times together on little weekend excursions and were guilty of the occasional sleepover, but all this was completely frowned upon by my traditional dad. Whenever we would embark on a trip, I would always first be subjected to the talk about how "it's-a no right," and how we "shouldn't be going away together," blah, blah, blah. He loved my husband from the beginning, but still, my dad is one stubborn Italian. (A stubborn Italian?! Shocking, I know.) Greg and I had planned a trip to Newport, Rhode Island, and I was procrastinating as much as possible on telling my dad. Finally, the day came for us to leave. My bag was packed and on my shoulder, and I was on my way out the door when I heard the dreaded: "Wherrrre you go?" I stopped in my tracks.

"Oh, um…to Rhode Island. Uh, with Greg. We'll be back Sunday night." I held my breath, shut my eyes tight, and waited. There was a long pause.

And then: "Oh. Okay. Have-a fun. Give me a kiss." I opened one eye, reluctantly leaned in for a quick peck, and then headed out the door. I paused on my front step after closing the door behind me. I breathed a sigh of relief that I had made it out unscathed from "the lecture."

There, in that moment, I reflected on how easy it was for me to scoot by my father for a weekend getaway with my boyfriend. Then, I half-shit my pants and half-smiled as it dawned on me: I was getting engaged this weekend, and that sneaky bastard knew.

Speaking of shitting your pants, Greg was a nervous wreck all weekend. In fact, he was so nervous that when we embarked on our walk down toward the rocks on the ocean, where he would pop the question, he had to turn around halfway so he could run back up to our room and…make a deposit. Nerves can be a real bitch.

We eventually got back on track, and headed down to the ocean. It was a beautiful, crisp fall day, without a cloud in the sky, the type of day where you were perfectly comfortable wearing a thin, long-sleeved t-shirt. We stood there on the rocks, watching the waves lazily bounce off the shore, and after a talk about our relationship and how happy we were together, he popped the question. It was magical, heartfelt, amazing – and so bizarre. Did this really just happen?!

You sort of have a picture in your head of how it may go down, what you'll be thinking, where, when, how and why. And then it happens. And it's happening in slow motion, yet it's too fast for the pace your brain wants it to be, and before you know it, you're hugging and kissing, wearing a ring, and nearby foreign tourists are snapping pictures and giving you the thumbs up (well, maybe that was just us). But either way, it's surreal.

Give Me an "E" for "Enjoyment"

We stood there for a while, soaking up the view. We were smiling, happy, and insanely excited. We eventually both reached for our phones. "Wait," I said. "Let's just sit here and enjoy this for a minute."

Of course, I was excited to call my mom and dad, his mom and dad, grandparents, all of our siblings, the Pope, my fourth grade math teacher, and everyone else under the sun, and so was my new fiancé. But I hesitated. It had nothing to do with anyone or anything in particular. But right then and there, it was just us. For that brief moment in time, we were engaged, no one knew yet, and it was quiet. Serene. Intimate. And I wanted to enjoy that for a minute.

I don't think I fully understood at the time why I felt this way, but something inside of me knew that once we said it out loud and let the news out, there would be strings attached. Plans would need to be made. Money would be involved. People would start asking questions.

We eventually did call our families and share the news, and it was amazing. But as the news spread further, the questions started flooding in, and the pressure was on. When would we get married? Where? What type of wedding would we have? Would we register for 300 or 20,000 thread count sheets? Would our Viennese hour be on the dance floor or in a separate room? Would I get laser hair removal? A bra to prevent backfat? Would there be enough seating in the cocktail hour? Would we want kids right away? Pandora would open up her tiny box, and that stubborn little bitch wouldn't close it up ever again.

It seemed like an overwhelming amount of decisions. All of this, just to say "I do"? All of this, just so I can get on with spending the rest of my life with my best friend? I was ready for the marriage. But I wasn't ready for the wedding.

I understand that not everyone feels this way. Some women exit the womb sporting a garter. They spend their entire lives dreaming of their wedding day, and I think that is absolutely fine. Some women do not find the planning process stressful in the least. (Whatever drug those women are on, please tell me where I can get some.) But I can assure you, even for these women, wedding fever will have them begging for a Xanax and ordering straightjackets for certain family members faster than they can say "I do." It will also bring on a plethora of curveballs, chaos, and "coulda, shoulda, woulda"'s of things they'd have done differently in hindsight, *if only they had been prepared.* My goal here is to make sure you, dear reader, are prepared.

Planning a wedding can be a great part about getting married – but it certainly shouldn't be the *best* part. Of course it is a wonderful time of your life, and certain aspects of planning can be fun. But brides: Take the time out to truly enjoy being engaged. Don't let anyone force you onto the merry-go-round of wedding planning at any pace other than your own.

Stores will tell you to hurry up and register, dress shops will say you must order your gown right now. Family may push you to get the ball rolling, and opinions and expectations will begin to creep in. For the most part, everyone means well, but it's just the nature of the beast that our society has created.

As women, we are socialized to be nice and have our shit together at all times, and usually the bulk of the coordinating falls on our shoulders. But you will see as you get going with your planning that things can become overwhelming very quickly. So don't be afraid to take your time. You have every right to slow it down, soak it in, and savor this period as much as you like. In fact, put that on your checklist of things to do.

Now that you've taken a deep breath…

Table #2:
Pre-Planning Checklist

Before you get on your way with cake tasting, gift registering and wedding kiss practicing, it's good to have a healthy dose of what marriage really is all about. You know, just so you have an idea of what you can expect. Doing so will help keep you grounded, and will further vaccinate you against crZybTch1 and its accompanying strains.

Prepare yourself for when the dust settles. Realize that when all of this silly bridal business is over you are likely going to be broke, tired and left to embark on the rest of your life with the person you chose to marry. And he is going to fart. A lot.

Oh, I know, that's not what you want to hear, but you better prepare yourself now for how to deal with this. No one ever tells you that the dainty little bite of cake you so gingerly feed him during your reception is actually only fart fuel that he will use to Dutch oven you at 3am.

Think that's gross? Well, it's reality, sister. And if this happens, you must take my advice and learn to fight back. Or take my grandma's advice: "Better out than in." Trust me on this one. You'll only need to dish out one *really* good one. Make sure you follow it up with an evil, dominant laugh. Nothing stops a man in his tracks faster than a fart from a female; they don't know how to process it. And as his brain begins to short circuit with fear, you will know you have found your weapon. Even though it should be funny, they can't laugh. Your husband will break wind with the best of them, but the moment his perfect little princess muffin lets one rip you'll see a look of utter confusion and terror cross his face. That's right: it's all fun and games until your man discovers your ability to strike back. God may have given us delicate little flowers, but he also gave us asses of steel. Don't test us, boys. And ladies, remember: All it takes is one. Just be sure to save it for the right time, and don't go overboard, letting out what my husband calls the "fart that could end a marriage." You have to know just how far you can take things before someone gets hurt. Keep that arrow in your quiver for emergency use only.

Whew! I'm glad we got that out of the way. I wouldn't be fulfilling my duty to you as an author and post-bride without letting you in on this little nugget of wisdom. And now, let's clear the air with a few of the more serious things to think about before you start wedding planning…

Discuss Your Groom's Involvement

It's helpful before you start planning to have an idea of how much or how little your groom will be involved in the wedding planning process. Maybe you have visions of the two of you making every decision together, from invitation color palettes to china patterns to cake fillings, but your man doesn't have a clue or an interest in any of it. Or maybe you are ready to sprint out of the gate and start calling the shots solo, but your husband doesn't want to be left in the dust. Whatever your style may be, there is no right or wrong as long as you are both comfortable. Talk it out from the beginning so you both know where you stand. It's better to lay it all out early in the game so you know what to expect and don't wind up brawling later on. Everyone is different, so decide what you are comfortable with and go from there.

The Tough Questions

Before you go any further with planning your wedding, ask yourself some tough questions about your relationship to make sure you are making the right decision. Seriously.

Can you believe I'm even bringing this up? This is a wedding book! What an asshole I am! But this is major, so stay with me for a moment. Because when the camera flashes stop, when the band packs up, and when your cake goes sour, it will be only you and your spouse. And unfortunately, as crazy as it may sound, not many people spend a whole lot of time thinking about *that* during wedding planning.

The nature of weddings makes it very easy to overlook certain signs of possible disaster ahead because you consume yourself with the planning aspect. You've got your brand new bling on your finger, and the circus of attention that comes along with an engagement has been swirling around you since your announcement. It's tempting to drink your own Kool-Aid and see the world through rose-colored, diamond-encrusted glasses. And on many levels, you should. But think very hard for a moment about the fact that once your wedding is over, you will be *spending the rest of your life with this person.* And with a quick glance at statistics, you will see that things come up that cause a lot of people to go back on their word. Life happens. True colors come out. People annul their marriage after seventy-two days. *Shit happens.*

During my writing and researching process, several realities of relationships emerged from those who were kind enough to share their stories with me. While no one wants to invite Debbie Downer to the wedding, I wouldn't be able to present this book to you in its most complete, honest form without saving her a seat at this table.

So hold tight as we pummel through this section, and conjure up your inner realist. When we're done, we can call security and have them kick the bitch out of the party.

Me, Two Therapists, a Mediator, and a Runaway Groom

No, that's not the title of a bad porno. It's simply four different types of people, each with its own personal set of questions you should ask yourself and warning signs you should read before saying "I do."

First, here are *my* recommendations of questions to ask before taking the plunge:

1. **Do you both agree on the idea of having children?** You'd be surprised at how many people don't talk about this before tying the knot, and spend years brawling about it later.

2. **Is he (or she) understanding and thoughtful?** Sensitive? Easy to be around? Or does he or she push people around?

3. **Is selfishness an issue?** Hopefully both of your needs in the relationship are being met. If you're always bending for someone else and they aren't doing the same for you, this can become a real problem.

4. **Is your fiancé gentle with others' feelings?** You've heard people say it before: "I'd never want to get on that guy (or girl's) bad side." If you're involved with that guy or girl, you may feel fortunate that you are part of their inner circle. But what if someone down the road changes sides? It's amazing and quite baffling at how quickly you could find yourself on the other side of the fence.

5. **Does he have homosexual tendencies?** (Same-sex brides: does *she* have straight ones?)

Then there are the "warning signs" from some of the therapists and mediators I interviewed. They recommend paying close attention to:

1. **If one person seems to be in a big hurry to marry.** (Laura Lawson, Clinical Social Worker/Therapist)

2. **If you find yourself censoring information** to friends about your partner, or sugar-coating things about him or her to your family. Likewise, if you find yourself censoring information about your life to your partner (Laura Frohboese, MSW, LSCW)

3. **If your partner isn't willing to go to a marriage enrichment course.** "These are often required through your church if you follow a particular religion, but even if you are not religious, you should still both be willing to attend a course like this before you marry." (Scott Hardy, Certified Divorce Mediator)

You may be asking: Why do I bring all this up? It's not to pee on your parade, I can assure you. It's to make sure you think about all of these things before you pull the trigger and saunter down the aisle in your over-priced gown. It's to bring a sense of reality into your life at a time when it's easy to get caught up in the fairy tale.

If your relationship is solid, then thinking about these things will only solidify it even further, and you have no need to worry. However, if your boat is a bit rocky, you may have some thinking to do. But rather than take my advice, or even the advice of professionals, let's ask someone who actually compiled for himself his own set of tough questions – and broke off his engagement before heading down the aisle.

George Was a Runaway Groom

"I've been engaged twice; once successfully, once in failure. As you might suspect, I get more questions about the one that failed than the one that succeeded. Typically, the questions come in the form of requests for advice on how to determine if getting married is the right thing to do. For the longest time I had trouble answering these questions; mostly because I did my best to block the whole thing out of my mind. But over the course of the past few years, I've allowed myself the opportunity to reflect on the misery that was my first engagement, and what I've come up with is a list of questions I think you should ask

yourself, should you be contemplating engagement, or if you are already engaged and you are questioning whether getting married is the right thing to do. But remember, if you want to come to a true conclusion, you need to answer these questions honestly. When it came to my first engagement, I realized I could not answer any of these questions in a manner that favored marriage and that is why my first engagement was not my last.

1. ***Do you want to get engaged (or did you get engaged) because you are absolutely in love with your significant other – or did you get engaged because it seemed like the next logical step in the relationship?*** *Really think about this answer. This is the most important question you can ask and the most difficult to answer honestly.*

2. ***Are most of your conversations with your partner confrontational?*** *If you are already engaged, and your answer to this question is yes, it could be because most of your conversations involve making decisions about the wedding (which typically involves spending a lot of money and therefore can be stressful). That in mind, try to think back to before you were engaged.*

3. ***Do you have fun when you are with your partner?***

4. ***Do you have more fun when you are not with your partner?***

5. ***Do you like your partner's personality?***

6. ***Do you find your partner physically attractive?***

7. ***Do you dislike most of your future in-laws?***

8. ***Do you get the sense that most of your future in-laws dislike you?***

9. ***Do you get the sense that your family/friends dislike your partner?***

10. ***Do you get the sense that your future partner dislikes your family and friends?***

11. *Do you get to spend a reasonable amount of time away from your partner, without your partner making you feel bad about it?*

12. *Do you get to spend time with your friends, without your partner?*

13. *Think about the things you like and dislike about your partner and make a determination on whether or not the likes outweigh the dislikes.*

14. *In stark contrast to the first question, the last question is the easiest question to answer, but still quite important. I put it last, because it marks the nail in the coffin to my first engagement. When your partner calls, and you see her (or his) name appear on your cell phone, do you get the unending urge to throw your phone across the room?*

Your answers to some of these questions individually can probably help you draw a pretty decisive conclusion to the question of whether or not you should get engaged (or move forward with your wedding), but certainly, the aggregate of most, or all of your answers will get you there.

As for me, contrary to my first engagement, my answers to these questions pertaining to my second engagement all favored marriage. Granted, I've only been married a few years, but it's been great so far. Of course, I'm not saying these questions will predict if you will have a happy marriage, but I believe they can help you determine if you'll have an unhappy one. And if these questions serve to help just one person make the right decision, it was worth the write."

Of course, there are things that are out of your control, and it's not possible to foresee everything coming your way. But if tiny little voices nag you every so often, tugging at your gut-strings, listen to them. I'm not talking about the voices that are pissed that your man didn't pick his socks up off the floor, or put the seat down on the toilet. I'm referring to the ones that are talking about his character and your compatibility. You need to open your ears for those.

Don't ignore your gut

Many of the therapists I met with while writing this book specialize in areas such as marriage counseling, group therapy and couples counseling. They all offered very insightful glances into the realities of relationships and all of the complexities involved (more on this later). But what I found very interesting is that, when working with women going through a divorce, these therapists have all heard the same thing from their clients: "I knew when I was walking down the aisle that I was making a mistake." So, why did they go through with it?

For many of them, the reason they admitted (in hindsight) is that the thought of the "wedding" somehow overshadowed the reality of the "marriage." For these women, it wasn't so blatantly obvious at the time. There was no movie moment, where an ex-lover stood up and yelled "I will not forever hold my peace!" or any type of revelation that occurred during the planning process. Instead, it was a tiny little tug on their gut strings that told them that something didn't feel right. And the majority concluded that if they hadn't been so focused on planning their wedding, they may have felt that tug a bit sooner.

As Licensed Professional Counselor Leslie Petruk puts it: "Many people spend more time talking about the wedding and planning for the wedding, way more than they do the relationship…these life-long things, they have spent little to no time talking about, but a day, they have spent hours and hours talking about – and fighting about, often times…"

Maybe this is not you, in which case, *wonderful*. I grant you full permission to skip on down to the next section. I hope that the majority of individuals planning a wedding are already certain that they have found their partner for life.

However, if this *is* you, and you have acknowledged these signs, you may want to pull up a chair.

You might be asking yourself: How could I go back on my word *now*? Maybe your concern is that the dress has been ordered, the reception hall is booked, or the invitations have already gone out. Maybe you just put a deposit down on the honeymoon. You're scared to tell the guests. You're walking down the aisle. The list goes on, and on, and on.

Now stop and think about the irony here: these are all material things. The only thing that is not material, the one thing that actually matters here, is your relationship and your life when you wake up tomorrow – which is possibly being swept under the rug for the sake of a four-hour party.

Lori, a great friend of mine and mother of two, sees how easy it is to get so caught up in wedding planning that you ignore red flags in a relationship. She offers this advice to her kids: "I tell them that it is never too late to honor that voice inside which is persistently saying 'no!' (assuming that is what's happening), and that it's not too late to change your mind even when you are halfway down the aisle. It is much worse to go forward into a marriage despite intuition which warns you not to disrupt a wedding ceremony."

In a nutshell, during your wedding planning hoopla, always pay attention to what's going on inside of *you*. Be careful that you are not committing to walking down the aisle because you are at a time in your life when you feel like you should. As therapist Laura Lawson puts it, "Some couples fall into marriage, rather than fall into love."

And if you do find yourself admitting that maybe you got caught up in the idea of a wedding and that this relationship is not right for you, listen to your gut and move on. You will find someone else, and you deserve to be happy. We all do. As stated by therapist Laura Frohboese: "There are no bad people, just bad matches." Take a good look at your own personal match. Make sure you aren't so set on saying "I do" that you find yourself saying, "He'll do," because that's not fair to either one of you. Don't plan to marry someone because he's a "great catch," he has what everyone around you wants, or he has all of the so-called qualities that you have plugged into a specific formula. He may look great on paper, but if your heart is not in it, you are only cheating yourself.

On the other hand, don't turn down the man that your heart loves because he doesn't hit your every mark. Many women wait around for the absolute perfect man. There are also a lot of people who wait in the woods for Bigfoot. Trust me, ladies – he's not coming, and there are very few women who claim to have spotted this beast. Instead of searching for the perfect man with the perfect qualities, search for the man that you feel wonderful around. This is the man with whom you have chemistry. He'll be caring and honest, with himself as well as with you, and that is the foundation for all great relationships. He'll have a big heart (and hopefully a big penis). And he'll be eager to grow (hopefully his penis will too). And, if *those* qualities are in place, you'll make it through anything.

Budget

Now that you have decided you want to get married, it is time to think about your budget. Some couples are great with their budget, and both individuals are rational and responsible when it comes to spending. For other couples, one person may be great with money, while the other waits for their partner to fall asleep so they can smuggle their purchases into the house and then pretend they were there the whole time. And for some couples, neither can list finances as a strong point. But when it comes to wedding planning, someone needs to be willing to step up to the plate. There are several expenses to factor in and, while some are obvious, plenty of others will creep up behind you and kick you in the bustle.

The number of free sites that will help you budget for your big day has grown tremendously. It doesn't matter which one you pick, so do some light research, narrow it down to one and stick with it. Some places that you may be registered may offer a tool that helps you budget right on their website. Whichever tool you choose, utilize it, as things can get out of hand very quickly.

Some of the more obvious costs to factor in your budget:

-Reception*
-Dress
-Music (ceremony, reception, cocktail hour)
-Flowers/decorations
-Photographer
-Videographer
-Attire
-Transportation
-Invitations (don't forget to include stamps, both for the invite and the
 RSVP card)
-Favors
-Honeymoon

*For the reception, be sure you know exactly what is included in the price of your hall. For further details, please see "Reception" table.

Some not-so-obvious fees that may creep up on you:

-Ceremony site fee
-Wedding rings
-Under garments
-Seating cards/chart
-Attendant gifts
-Fee for taking pictures at a particular site (if applicable)
-Gratuities for vendors, maître de, and/or bridal attendant

And on, and on, and on. Every wedding is of course different, so you may have more or less, but think it through before you start booking anything so that you are well-prepared. The last thing you need while coordinating your wedding is to start fighting over unbudgeted expenses.

Open Discussion

Before you jump headfirst into planning, set a date night with your future hubby. Light some candles, pour some wine, play some Barry White…and lay your financial cards out on the table.

Sexy, right? I know. But this is crucial, and it's one of the most important things you can do to protect yourself from problems down the road. If you don't address your finances and come clean about debt, it will negatively affect your relationship. Take some advice from Suze Orman, as she shared to *O, The Oprah Magazine*:

"You must talk money before your relationship becomes serious – a person's financial habits are an incredible insight into his values and ethics. That doesn't mean a lousy credit score is a reason to break up, but if you find that your new love interest doesn't handle money responsibly, you have to question what else he isn't going to be upright about. If you're the one with the issues, be honest about your shortcomings. A good relationship is one in which each party helps the other make better choices – and you and your beau might be able to help each other become smarter about money."

Being open and honest about your finances can also create a mutual respect and understanding for each other, and will allow you to figure out the best way to handle them once you are married. One of the best (and in my humble opinion, most healthy) ways to do this is to each keep individual bank accounts, and create one joint account to which you will both contribute. Explains Suze:

"Once you've determined the total cost of your shared living expenses, both of you should contribute your portion of these costs to the joint account each month, based on your share of the household income. (For example, if you make $60,000 and your partner makes $40,000, you're responsible for 60 percent of household expenses.) Whatever money doesn't go toward these costs stays in the individual accounts, to be used at each person's discretion."

While the above may not work for everyone, it can certainly work for many. Personally, this works great for me and Greg. And because I completely suck at remembering to transfer money into the joint account after every paycheck, I just set up my account so that every time I get paid, a set amount is automatically transferred.

At this point, you're hopefully relaxing and enjoying being engaged. You know you want to get married, you are on the same page with your budget, and are off to a great start. It's time to move on to table #3...

Table #3:
The Bridal Party

The question will arise as to whether or not you should have a bridal party. Prior to making any big decisions, take a step back and look at the scenario from a few different angles. Remember, you are excited, it's a fun time, and you may want to stand on a mountain and ask the world. But truly consider whom you want to give the honor of being a part of your special day before you make any moves.

Susan Has Regrets

"Really think about who is in your wedding party – don't just fill in people because you need an even number of friends or family members standing at the altar with you. I had a bridesmaid who was a fairly new 'friend' - and I use the term 'friend' loosely! She felt like this event was all about her. She spent the whole weekend being critical of everyone – including our parents! Some of this I witnessed and was able to just brush it off, but a lot of it was shouldered by my absolutely wonderful maid of honor. So the lesson is this: if there is someone in your bridal party that could potentially behave inappropriately, make sure

there is someone in the bridal party to balance it out. My maid of honor covered up so much of the bad behavior, I had no idea it was going on until I came back from my honeymoon. I realize how unfair this was to my maid of honor, and had I known about it, I certainly would have asked the venue to escort the bridesmaid out of the building and instructed them she was not to return. Be prepared for this and how you would deal (and if you even want to). It sucks to think about, but so many people have horror stories about people like this."

While Susan put someone in her wedding that she did not know too well at the time, and suffered the consequences, other brides found themselves unpleasantly surprised when they invited a close friend or family member to be in their bridal party who unexpectedly acted out as well.

For instance, one of Tonya's bridesmaids, whom she considered a "very good friend," pitched a fit right before they were to go to the church – because she was having a bad hair day. Seriously. There was really nothing wrong with her hair, other than the fact that it didn't come out exactly as she expected. Tonya and the other girls tried to reassure her that it was fine, and that they needed to hurry and get on the bus so they could get to the church. (To make matters worse, the bridesmaid in question waited until the last possible second to get her hair done in the first place, despite the other girls urging her to get started.) But instead of pulling up her big girl panties and remembering that the day was about her friend and not her, she made the stylist take down her hair and start over - while the bride and other bridesmaids waited for her on the bus.

Best of the Best, Worst of the Worst

You think you know people - until you plan a wedding. I'm not sure if it's because of all the emotions involved, or the anticipation of the event, or the stress of the roles everyone tries to determine they will play. Maybe it's a combination of everything. But emotions and sensitivity often run high at weddings, and this can be a very good thing or a very bad thing.

For instance, I have a friend who never had a great relationship with her mother (in fact, "derailed roller-coaster ride" would be a better description). But when my friend got engaged, it solidified a bond between the two of them, and her mother has been an absolute dream ever since. Maybe she has become sentimental, and the marriage has finally allowed her to see her daughter as an adult. Or maybe my friend was just able to relate to her mother in a way she never could until now. Whatever the case, the wedding planning and marriage has seemed to open doors and fix something that was broken for a very long time, and that is a beautiful thing.

However, others have much different stories. I know one bride whose parents were bitterly divorced several years ago, and were using their daughter's wedding as a parental pissing contest; another whose crazy and insecure mother-in-law was shelling out Benjamins like tic-tacs just so she could control and take ownership of every little decision the couple was making; and even another whose jealous bridesmaid was an obnoxious brat the entire day since it wasn't about her, going out of her way to have a bad time and even sneaking out of the wedding early without even saying goodbye to the bride and groom. It's amazing what weddings can stir up in people.

One thing is for sure: my mom has always been right on the money when she says, "Weddings bring out the best of the best, and the worst of the worst." And no matter what type of wedding you are planning, chances are you will come across some bad behavior. So give the bridal party *a lot* of thought before you jump in and decide on who will play an important role in your day.

The other side of the fence

Maybe you've read the above, and have also taken into consideration the experiences from others in your own life, but you decide that you do in fact have a solid group that will make this event positive, fun and stress-free. But before you seal the deal, consider that you may still open yourself up to drama from those you are *not* asking. Our next bride, Elizabeth, learned this the hard way. Her story:

"Friends and family were always an extremely important part of our lives, so selecting our wedding party was naturally one of the first steps in our wedding planning process. The most obvious choices were having my younger sister as my Maid of Honor and my long-time best friend as a bridesmaid. I also knew that I wanted to have my future sister-in-law as a bridesmaid. After being in a sorority in college, there were many women who I was extremely close friends with; however, there were three women in particular who stood out to me within this group, who I eventually would call my bridesmaids. There you have it: one Maid of Honor and five bridesmaids. Naturally, it took my husband (then, fiancé) about five minutes to decide who he wanted as his Best Men (he had two) and groomsmen. Typical. Our wedding party selection was complete, and we couldn't be happier with our decisions! If only everyone in our lives felt this way.

As Facebook is becoming more and more prevalent in our everyday lives, my Maid of Honor and bridesmaids decided (with my permission, of course) to post on Facebook how happy and honored they were to be asked to be a bridesmaid in my wedding. I thought it was cute and harmless. Boy, was I wrong. A few days had passed since the girls posted this on Facebook, and I had a lunch date with a few sorority sisters, one of which was a bridesmaid. One of my friends at lunch seemed really disengaged and in a foul mood, which was completely uncharacteristic of her. She is normally loud, bubbly, and always cracking jokes. On this day, however, she was stand off-ish and kind of short-tempered, especially toward me. At first, I thought she was jealous that I was engaged and she wasn't because she had been talking for quite a while about how she wants her boyfriend to pop the question. Our lunch date had finally ended, and we all drove separately and were on our way home. My friend, who was also a bridesmaid, called me right when she got in her own car and explained to me why my one friend was in a bad mood during lunch. There were two reasons: 1) She was not asked to be a bridesmaid and 2) She had to find out via Facebook that she wasn't asked to be a bridesmaid. Funny, I never read in any wedding etiquette book that I should call and warn someone ahead of time that they were not going to be a bridesmaid. I must have skipped that chapter.

I was completely dumbfounded, and I could not believe that someone would have the gall to tell another (who was a bridesmaid) that they were upset that they were not a bridesmaid. In an event where someone should be happy and excited for a friend, they instead were just acting jealous. I just couldn't believe it, and I was a mixed bag of emotions at this point. Not only was I angry, but I also felt badly about hurting someone's feelings. I would never ever intend for that - ever. Later that day, my jealous friend text messaged me that she was sorry for acting "grumpy" during lunch, and that she thought we were close enough friends where she should have been a bridesmaid. To make a long story short, we both apologized and moved on with our lives. But, I will never ever forget that.

When a couple gets engaged, it's a joyous time for them. Although it is also exciting for those who are asked to be a part of the wedding party, the wedding itself is not about the wedding party. It's about the bride and groom and beginning their lives as a married couple, not about a bridesmaid celebrating being a bridesmaid."

Have you figured out by now that there is truth in the expression: "Weddings aren't about the bride and the groom"? Some people just can't be happy for you. They will stomp and cry, throw a bitch fit, and will always, always, always make it about them.

Think about how your vendors will be affected

Aside from the people you may be choosing, you may also want to think about how having a bridal party affects the vendors you choose. For my own wedding, we had ten bridesmaids and ten groomsmen. My sister and her husband, on the other hand, did not have a bridal party – they simply had one maid of honor (me) and one best man (the groom's brother). I remember how relieved her photographer was that there were not a slew of people involved in her day, because it allowed him to spend time with and focus on her and her groom. He went on to describe how difficult it is to coordinate with a large group of people, and how it cuts into the time he could be using to get great shots of the happy couple. While a big group can be fun to party with, you may lose a little of the intimacy with those most special to you along the way. If you do decide on a bridal party, make sure you are confident your vendors know how to work with large groups.

As you weigh your decision, try not to feel any pressure to have a bridal party if you aren't feeling it. It's okay to opt-out. Don't worry about hurting people's feelings, because they'll get over it. Remember, the VIPs in your life, whom you love dearly and who are happy for you, will be a part of your wedding, regardless as to whether or not you pick out what dress or tux they will wear. It would just happen naturally. For example: my sister-in-law and her husband did not have a bridal party, but they were surrounded by everyone who loved and cared about them, and their destination wedding was an absolute blast. She asked me to do her hair for her and help her get ready, and I was honored. It meant the world to me, and proved that I didn't need to be carrying a bouquet or walking down the aisle before her to show her that I cared.

Also remember when you ask a large group of men or women to play a role in your day, you will now have to manage many different personalities, and coordinating them will become a bigger job. As much as you would like to believe that everyone will be responsible, helpful and cooperative, count on the fact that certain people will sadly always bring their drama. You don't want to look back at those panoramic shots of your bridal party and see any wolves in sheep's clothing.

This is not to say that everyone is like this. If you have a wonderful and solid group of close friends who you know in your heart of hearts will make this a fun, happy and positive experience, then go for it. Don't let a few bad apples spoil the bunch. Just be sure you are not putting anyone in your party for the sake of obligation, because you are only creating added stress for yourself. Overall we had a great time with our large wedding party and were thankful for the friends and family who shared that day with us. But looking back, we realized that most would have stepped up for us no matter what – bridal party or no bridal party.

One final note to consider before you make your decision: Looking back on my wedding planning regarding the bridal party, I realized that there was so much to do that I hadn't considered beforehand. Coordinating dress/tux fittings, relaying information, putting together a rehearsal dinner, purchasing gifts – the list goes on and on. And, as in Susan's case mentioned above, your maid of honor may bear the brunt of any antics that take place along the way.

I also realized that being a bridesmaid for someone has its own laundry list of money to spend and things to do. I tried my best not to put anyone out, and I believe they noticed and were thankful for that. But just the commitment alone required time and money spent on their part, which I know is precious to all of us. They would have loved me just the same, bridesmaid or no bridesmaid. Who knows, maybe some of them would have even been relieved to not have been asked. I acknowledge this in a positive light – I know it does not mean they don't love me, aren't happy for me and excited for me, and didn't wish me well. It's just the nature of the situation. But my overall point is this: If you have a big bridal party, you may find yourself worrying so much about everyone else that you take time away from you and your husband. Because after all, that's who the wedding is all about – at least, it should be.

Bridesmaids: Things You Should Know

If you are a bridesmaid, let's discuss a bit of bridesmaid communication etiquette, shall we? Everyone knows we are all busy and, especially for us women, we have several balls up in the air at once. But keep in mind that when you agree to be a bridesmaid or maid of honor in someone else's wedding, you are committing yourself on some level to be involved in whatever takes place. There are a lot of moving parts in planning a wedding, and sometimes a bride is waiting on her bridesmaids to answer a question or give her feedback on something and she can't move forward until she gets a reply.

Now let's be clear: I'm not talking about Psycho Suzie, the bride who emails you forty-five times a day to tell you the shade your shoes must be dyed and how many times you can blink while walking down the aisle. That bitch needs to check herself in while simultaneously registering at Target for a life. I'm talking about the bride who occasionally sends you an email wanting to know things like whether or not you and your date plan on spending the night so she can block off the right amount of hotel rooms; or the maid of honor who just needs an idea if you are in or out for the bachelorette party so she can plan accordingly. Maybe shoot your girl an email if you haven't heard from her in a while to see if she needs anything, or how she's holding up - that sort of thing. Some brides have a hard time asking for help because they don't want to put anyone out, and many won't even accept the help when offered. But a simple phone call or gesture of care can go a long way, and even the mere offer can alleviate some pressure.

If you receive correspondence from the bride or maid of honor, just answer the damn email, even if it's just to say that you need a little more time to answer. Be considerate. If you start complaining that you don't have time, then you should really think about how important being in this wedding is for you. Any sane bride will tell you that she'd understand if you declined to be in the wedding (when asked or shortly after, of course; not a month before the wedding), due to reasons such as financial obligations, or because you have a crazy year and just can't swing it. Politely declining is much better than rudely accepting and pretending you are too good to participate, or complaining about everything along the way.

That said: brides, be careful of demanding too much of your girls. I know it's stressful when you are planning your wedding, but remember: tons of bitches do this every day. Your bridesmaids have lives and are busy, and while they want what's best for you and wish you nothing but happiness, they are not and should not be treated as if they are your personal assistants, sitting at their computers, hands on the home keys, waiting for your demands to come pouring into their inboxes. They have papers due. Kids with poo in their diapers. Episodes of *Real Housewives* to catch up on. Chill the fuck out.

You should also keep in mind what you are asking of someone when you enlist them as a bridesmaid. They now have an obligation to invest in you with both time and money: bridal shower, bachelorette party, gifts and possible travel, in addition to every little piece of penis paraphernalia that goes along for the ride; not to mention the overpriced dress, hair, makeup and accessories. They may have several weddings in one year in which they are involved aside from yours. Be considerate, and be thankful.

Be confident, as well. Don't be that bride that puts her girls in heinous dresses so no one "upstages" her. Remember how Kate Middleton had her sister/maid of honor, Pippa, wear a white dress for her wedding to Prince William? I know what you're thinking: Who the fuck names their kid Pippa? But that's beside the point. The bride *asked her to wear white*. Sure, that's a bit extreme. But that, my friends, is one confident bitch.

Bridesmaids: Be Mindful of Time Frames

When the bride needs you to do something by a certain time, such as having you measured for your dress, just get it done. Don't make her call you or stay on your back until you get it together. Usually all of the bridesmaid's dresses need to be ordered at the same time, to ensure you receive a group discount or so that the colors match properly or because the people at the bridal shop are being total Nazis about the whole damn thing. If your measurements aren't in, you could hold up the whole group.

Try to remember that while this is an exciting time for your friend, it can also be a very stressful time for her, and she may be a bit on edge. Give her the occasional free pass and do your best to cooperate. And bridesmaids, while you're here, let's go over one more thing…

Clinical Definition of catatonic:

n.

An abnormal condition variously characterized by stupor, stereotypy, mania, and either rigidity or extreme flexibility of the limbs. It is most often associated with schizophrenia.

Please see: face of a bridesmaid walking down the aisle at a wedding.

The bride tells you what dress to get, maybe picks out your shoes, and buys you a nice piece of jewelry. Heck, she may even throw in a mani/pedi, or pay for your hair. No matter how much you think you are prepared, NO ONE informs you of the deer-in-headlights impulse that instinctually occurs the second those church doors open and you are sent on your own down the Aisle of Judgment. Your legs are moving, but that's about all you can control, and as a result, you appear in pictures as if you swallowed a series of pain meds and washed it down with a mimosa.

Do not let this be you. Sure, it's not about you - it is about the bride, of course – which means you should do your best to smile like a normal person as you pave the way for her. Do what it takes beforehand to prepare yourself. Try as best you can to ignore the pressure of walking in six inch stilettos all by yourself with three cans worth of hairspray in your perfectly coiffed hair while holding a ten-pound bouquet and sweating from every orifice in front of complete and total strangers while trying simultaneously not to trip on the custom-made aisle runner or clumsy photographer. No problem, right?

While some girls are seasoned veterans at this, for others, it always brings on the stress. Instead of focusing on the aforementioned, here are some tips on appearing as natural as possible in this situation:

*__Try to imagine__ a dear friend or loving family member, and hopefully this will conjure up a somewhat relaxed-looking smile as you saunter down the aisle.

***Know your role**. You are here for the bride. Pay attention at the rehearsal so you know where to go on the big day and can confidently get there.

***Slow it down**. The faster you walk, the more likely you are to trip or look like a maniac.

***Do a boob check** before you head down the aisle. A funny little thing about those expensive dresses is that they are often manufactured pretty cheaply, so make sure your girls are pulled and tucked. You don't want to signal the arrival of the beautiful bride with your Bouncy Boobies Day Parade.

***For god's sake, eat something before the ceremony**. Eating will make you less shaky and put some color in your cheeks. Save the white for the bride's dress.

Things a Groomsman Should Know

Rent a cheap tux. Show up. (I hate you.)

Bridal Party Gift Giving

It's customary to give gifts to your bridal party as a "thank you" for being in your wedding. This is usually done at the rehearsal dinner. You can give many different types of gifts, but if I could make one suggestion, it would be to add a personal touch. Don't let this be an afterthought. Again, people are putting themselves out for you and this is an opportunity to show your gratitude.

Everyone's style is different, but I am not a fan of simply giving a necklace or pair of earrings that you expect the bridesmaids to wear for your wedding. I say this because it's not really a "gift" in the sense that they may not like it, and if that's the case, they can't really use it after your day has passed.

How about letting them wear their own jewelry and instead giving them gift certificates to the spa? Or maybe get them all a personalized tote, and fill it with inexpensive but thoughtful goodies. When it came time to give my bridesmaids a gift, I made them personalized gift bags filled with things I thought they would like. They all were essentially the same, but each gift had a unique touch that was tailored specifically to each girl. Every bag contained:

*a beautiful shawl (colors differed for each girl).

*a compact mirror from Brighton, with a cute pic of the bridesmaid and myself in it (of course they could change this out, but just for the novelty of the gift, it worked).

*a pair of earrings (the same for each girl, but there was no obligation to wear them for our wedding day. I happen to know a woman who makes custom jewelry and I worked with her to design a pair I thought my girls would like).

*a "purse hook," a bling'd out version of the kind that allows you to hang your purse off of any table or bar so that it does not have to go on the floor.

I placed all of the items in a gift bag, and used the purse hook to hang it from their spot at the table. In total, I spent around $75 on each girl. You certainly do not have to do that – maybe $50 is your magic number, or even $25. Just put some time into it, work it into your budget early on, and don't leave it as an afterthought.

Guys, some great ideas for your groomsmen are:

*tickets to a sporting event
*a jersey of their favorite team or player
*a gift card
*a techie gift (i.e.: solar radio, Star Wars flash drive, etc.)

The possibilities are endless. For our wedding, my husband got each of his guys a monogrammed money holder, and put a gift card inside. Again - personal and thoughtful. My best friend's husband got his guys old-fashioned monogrammed pocket watches – I thought that was a great gift, and very different.

Here are some sites to get you brainstorming on bridal party gift ideas:

*www.etsy.com – If you haven't discovered Etsy by now, get on it. They have all things handmade, and you can find some really cool stuff. (They recently also launched a "Wedding" website.)
*www.mulberrymoon.com
*www.redenvelope.com
*www.shoploveme.com
*www.uncommongoods.com
*www.weddingish.com

More Bridal Party Shenanigans: Clink, clink, clink! I'd like to propose a toast

If you are a maid of honor or best man and will be giving a speech, one of the best pieces of advice out there is to remember to KISS the bride and groom. That means **K**eep **I**t **S**imple, **S**tupid.

The best speeches are usually short and sweet, from the heart, and not read off of a piece of paper. Now everyone, of course, has their own personal definition of "simple." I broke my own rule on this one when giving a speech at my sister's wedding; I brought a "cheat sheet" up with me because I had certain points I wanted to be sure I made, but I was careful not to sound like a robot. The best man for this wedding broke this rule as well by reading from a piece of paper, but it worked for him and he absolutely killed it. Just do what feels right for you.

But whatever you do, put some thought into it beforehand. From the weddings I've been to over the past few years, I will say the following: Best Men, don't get up there and talk about how the first time you met your bro's wifey was during her walk-of-shame leaving his apartment one morning. Maids of Honor, don't ever refer to your newly-married sister's ecstatic smile as resembling "Mr. Ed" while holding a microphone in front of three hundred people. I don't care if that was the loving and affectionate nickname you gave to her after she saved you by pulling you out of that river near the horse fields as a child – now is not the time. Save it for the card.

If you know the bride/groom has a great sense of humor, leave the personal digs and one-night stand tales for the bachelor/bachelorette parties, where you could maybe do a "roast." If you truly can't say anything nice, politely let the bride and groom know ahead of time that you will be opting out of the speech. There's no law that says you have to get up there in the first place.

Hopefully you now have a clearer picture of the pros and cons of having a bridal party. I can only hope to prepare you for what's to come so that you can handle it appropriately, make the best decisions, and get on with your life. Because really, isn't this wedding supposed to be about you, your future spouse, and your life together?

Whatever you choose, make sure that whomever you ask to be a part of this special day is someone you hold near and dear, and who truly deserves the honor. And if you're not feeling it, don't be afraid to take a stand and say no to the shenanigans.

Now, time to tackle some of the family. Let's head over to Table #4…

Table #4:
The In-Laws & Other
Family Members

Dealing with in-laws can be the number-one stressor in a marriage, right up there with finances. It's pretty likely that if you are in a relationship with someone, you have felt the ~~wrath~~ stress of this person's family at some point, on some level. While communication in your marriage is key, the need to communicate does not stop at your spouse. You need to learn and be prepared to communicate with each other's families as well. Honing this skill will strengthen your marriage and keep you out of harm's way.

I don't know if the gods smiled upon me when Greg and I met, or if I did some wonderful deed that I have long since forgotten, but I consider myself insanely lucky in the in-law department. My husband comes from a big family, and I can say with honesty that I love them all - including my mother-in-law. I think that part of this comes from the fact that they are an amazing group of people, but also because we all approach our relationships from a good place and we communicate. None of us are perfect, but ıone of us is here to attack each other or make each other's

.o also come clean and say that, with a couple of serious boy-friends I had before settling down with Greg, I dodged a few bullets in the mother-in-law department. There was one who was so overbearing that I was convinced her son was still breast-feeding after I left his house every night, and another who I never did get to meet in person, although the picture I found of her in my then-boyfriend's apartment with pencil holes drilled through the eyes did not exactly scream "World's Greatest Mom." So I consider myself very fortunate to have the relationship that I do with my in-laws. Because sometimes, in-laws can be downright scary – espe-cially come wedding season.

On Dealing with Toxic Family Members

We do what we can to surround ourselves with a great friend base and positive people. I firmly believe that we all come in and out of each other's lives for a reason, sometimes more than one, and that if we pay close atten-tion we can respect the fact that we are all in this life together, navigating our way through the unknown and searching to connect with each other, learn from each other, give from each other and take from each other.

I also know that sometimes, for no good reason, some people just sim-ply fucking suck.

The problem arises for many of us when people come into our lives that we don't get to choose. This happens in the form of in-laws, cousins, even siblings and parents. You love them, sure; but they are making you crazy and infringing on your mental health during one of the most impor-tant times of your life.

The bar for crazy is raised even higher when the word "wedding" is thrown into the mix: suddenly those that are the most volatile tend to back up for a running start and swan-dive right off into the deep end. So, rather than pay a stranger on a weekly basis to listen to your familial ramblings, or throw added stress onto an already hectic time, let's take a different approach.

Realize that the only thing we have control over is the way we *react* to said relative/soon-to-be-in-law. You may be thinking, "But…she is trying to control my entire wedding!" or "She is bullying me into making decisions I am not comfortable with!" or maybe "He expects me to do everything exactly like he did!" Yes, yes, and yes. But the bottom line is that people, whether subconscious or intentional, act like this because they have their own inner battles going on, they are trying to control you, they are desperate for attention and/or recognition, or they have some crazy need to be validated through you. Fortunately, none of these reasons are your problem, but *un*fortunately, they can still make you crazy.

Even if you know you are in the right, whether you blow up in their face or keep it all inside, it doesn't matter – they are *affecting* you and your well-being. And they aren't masterminds, so don't overestimate them. It's a natural reaction that they can't help but carry out.

The best thing you could do is tackle each issue separately as it arises, being firm but respectful, and to continue on with your planning process without paying their antics any attention. Eventually they will tire from your lack of notice and move on to other victims, because they aren't getting anywhere with you.

The trick is to disconnect yourself emotionally as much as possible from the person causing you harm, at least when regarding the particular situation. I know this sounds utterly impossible. But in order to keep yourself healthy, you need to hone these skills. And when it comes to in-laws that you have to encounter on a fairly regular basis, especially during wedding planning when it seems that everyone has an opinion, this is a necessary (albeit difficult) task. But you need to do so in order to avoid further conflict or resentment toward the particular family member.

"Harboring resentment is like drinking the poison in hopes that the other person will die." ~Author Unknown

We are the only ones who are hurt in the end when we hold grudges and harbor hatred. It can become especially difficult to let go when in-laws are involved, because these are people we did not choose, yet we must deal with them. And in doing so, we need to come to terms with some form of acceptance.

Unfortunately, acceptance does not mean you will hold hands, sing Kumbaya and bake chocolate chip cookies together every Saturday night. Sure, you can change your outlook and work on yourself, but in order for relationships to work, the other party needs to be just as willing, and often this is not the case. The person in question will most likely never change – and that's okay. We just need to exude confidence, figure out the best way to deal with them and happily go about our daily lives. If they continue to choose to be miserable, then so be it – as long as your own health is secure, it won't matter. And it's very important to acknowledge the fact that your health is literally at stake if you allow others to get your blood to boil. If you find yourself in this type of situation, trust me, you are not alone. Below, Madeline's story…

Madeline's Mother-in-Law

Here's my tale of the "CRAZY MIL FROM HELL THAT WANTS ALL THE RECOGNITION." Allow me to list the ways.

She wanted to walk my husband down the aisle. She hemmed and hawed and couldn't accept my husband's answer.

She jumped ON the altar after we were announced as husband & wife, and told my husband to give her a kiss. He looked at her like the crazy ass that she is, and said 'What? Why?' Her answer: 'Because I'm your mother'. He still shudders when we talk about it!

I have one regret: letting her affect me to the point of stomach pains & diarrhea leading up to the wedding. In fact, both my hubby & I hired a wedding planner purposely to keep her in check. She was in check...on the surface. But that did not stop her from muttering passive-aggressive comments under her breath. (Example: My husband's brother asked her at rehearsal dinner: "Mom, aren't you excited for the wedding?" Her answer: "Well, I guess since we are not included in anything it doesn't feel 'real' to me.") This crazy B contributed towards the reception hall only, and was included in all decisions regarding the hall, such as food, and seating!

She didn't even look at me on the wedding day - didn't tell me I looked nice or anything. Can you say, jealous, much? She gave me an attitude throughout the whole process...never acted excited, and was always trying to 'upstage' me (her words, not mine!).

She was annoyed that I would not include her in my gown shopping. Well, I had a legitimate reason: During the early stages of my search, I showed her a gown online that I really liked, and wanted to try on. She looks at the gown, then looks me up & down and says, 'Oh no, you are much too hippy for that'. Pick your jaw up, that is what she said. Mind you, she is quite overweight herself, and I am not.

So, therefore, I didn't want or need her negativity on what is supposed to be 'the happiest day'...blech."

Madeline has found herself in an unfortunate situation with her mother-in-law, and it clearly sucks. She could simply lie down and suffer, while simultaneously purchasing stock in Charmin to take care of that little stomach problem. Or she can remedy the situation by learning from someone who's been there.

Enter Mary Jo. A seasoned veteran, Mary Jo has endured years of mother-in-law issues that are eerily similar to young Madeline's. This year, Mary Jo celebrates 40 years of marriage – and along with that, she will celebrate her mother-in-law's one-hundredth birthday. Oh yes. This bitch knows what she's talking about.

Mary Jo will tell you that her success in dealing with her mother-in-law is one hundred percent attributed to how she *reacts* to her. Very early in her marriage, she realized two things: 1) that her mother-in-law was insanely difficult to deal with, and 2) that she cannot change her mother-in-law. This last realization, she swears, is the number-one element with which we all need to come to terms.

And she means *really* come to terms. Because there is a difference between *knowing* that we need to come to terms with an issue and *truly* coming to terms with said issue, and this is something of which we are all guilty at times. To fully understand that you cannot change another individual, no matter how good or bad you perceive them to be, is the first step in taking the stress away from yourself and your relationships.

While the antics unfolded over the years, ranging from minor offenses to severe familial crimes, Mary Jo states she would "… never, never, never do anything about it, because I put my husband first. He knew she was difficult. So why would I argue? It's not going to make her different."

That last sentence is the key. *It's not going to make her any different.* The only thing you have any control over is your reactions toward her and your own inner feelings. It may help to realize that, no matter how hard this may be to comprehend, she is not doing things to intentionally harm you. It's just in her nature to act a certain way, and you just so happen to be the woman who married her son, which of course puts you on the receiving end of her behavior. This is simply the person she is. Insert any woman into the equation, and her behavior would probably be no different.

In a nutshell, Mary Jo's advice is: "DEAL with it. You are not changing her. You'll never make her think the way you think. So why have a problem in *your* house because of it?"

She brings up an excellent point. When you harbor animosity toward your mother-in-law (or anyone, for that matter), you bring that energy and negativity into your own home. You are on edge and pissed off and, before you know it, you are fighting with your husband and you don't even know why.

Is this necessary? Of course not, and if you let this continue without acknowledging it and remedying the situation, you are placing a wedge between you and your husband. And that's no way to operate within a marriage.

When planning a wedding, try to avoid your mother-in-law's drama (or whomever you are dealing with) by not giving the attention she is probably searching for. When communicating, try to remain as neutral as possible, be as courteous as possible, and then do what you want to do for your day (without being spiteful or doing anything just because you know she wants the opposite). Stay true to your wedding day visions, and be grateful if she makes financial contributions. And if you truly clash on certain traditions or elements of your big day, try to find a way to pay for those elements yourself or with the help of your family, as this will ensure she cannot hold anything over your head and take control of something that means a great deal to you.

Remember, how you interact with her regarding your wedding will set the stage for your relationship throughout your entire marriage. Regardless of her actions, you have the power to make this relationship as bearable and stress-free as you can from this point in the game, so utilize this advice – because the wedding is just the beginning.

Your own family

You may be experiencing some push-back from your own family when it comes to planning your wedding. This can particularly be true if you are a bride who wants to do things a bit differently than what your own family expected.

In the end, you want to honor your family but make them understand that you are doing things a certain way because that is who you are, and that is what you and your fiancé want. You are not doing things to go against their wishes, or to hatch some plan you've plotted against them, or to break their hearts, or for any other reason. You can lighten things up by gently explaining this to them (and it won't hurt to keep them busy with other ways they can be a part of your day).

On the flip side, be sure you aren't trying so hard to do something different in order to make a statement of defiance. Weed all of that other crap out, and stick to your guns as to what you've always wanted and dreamed of.

In the years to come, that is the wedding you will always look back on with love and memories. As we can see in several examples throughout this book, you will never make everyone happy during your wedding planning. There's simply no way. So let it go from now, stay true to yourself, and worry about making only two people happy: you, and your fiancé.

The Little Things

Of course, not everyone has extreme issues with their family members and in-laws. Sometimes the instances are more subtle, but they do exist, and things can still become difficult. You're not going to see eye-to-eye on everything your spouse's family does, but you should, for your own family's sanity, work to maintain a level of respect. No matter how you slice it, if you aren't being respectful to your husband's family, then you aren't being respectful to your husband, and the same applies for how your husband treats your crazy-ass family (because we're all a little crazy, are we not?).

It doesn't matter who's right, who's wrong, or what was said or done. What matters is how you handle yourself, and your ability to *protect your marriage from stress*. Don't ever forget that protecting your marriage from stress should be your ultimate goal and concern, and any rifts involving family members on either of your sides can slowly creep in and affect the relationship you share with your spouse.

Maybe you have a problem with your mother-in-law, and maybe your husband agrees with you. Like Mary Jo's husband, he knows she's a handful. That's wonderful that he understands. Be thankful for this, and then move on, and don't use every opportunity to point out the obvious to him. Because no matter how much he agrees with you, she's still his mother, and there's only so much shit-talking a man can take.

To put this into perspective, take a glance from a different angle. Your mom somehow knows how to locate your last nerve and incessantly pluck it like a guitar string. She makes you nuts. You have a two-hour vent-fest to your husband as to why she irritates you and why you had to hang up on her because you just can't deal. The next night your husband mentions that your mom can be a real pain in the ass sometimes. Whoa, whoa – what?!? Now he's crossed the line.

See what I mean?

You don't need to love your in-laws. You don't even have to like them. Just figure out a way to make your encounters as pleasant as possible so you can all get on with your lives and stop wasting precious energy. (Remember, we may not have been their pick-of-the litter, either.) In the end, the more you allow yourself to be eaten up by the actions of your in-laws, no matter how hideous they are, the more you are hurting yourself and your family. You can love them from afar, if you have to, pulling back when necessary. And don't forget to always keep boundaries, because if you don't, nobody else will. No one should have a say in your marriage except for you and your husband.

It's also good to remember one important factor about your marriage: We women have so much power and influence over the men in our lives. Men don't want to admit this, but it's the truth. Sure, it may look like they are calling the shots and deciding things on their own, pounding on their chests as they go. But really, it's us women who are the driving forces. It's like the line in the movie "My Big Fat Greek Wedding," where the mother, Maria Portokalos, says to her daughter Toula: "Let me tell you something, Toula. The man is the head, but the woman is the neck. And she can turn the head any way she wants." This is a powerful tool and can be great in many ways, but if we are not careful, it can also be misused and cause serious destruction.

You may not like your husband's family. But please, unless they are all totally horrible, fire-breathing monsters causing you all serious pain, refrain from using your superpower to turn him away from them, or make him think less of them. Because you do have the ability to single-handedly place the wedge, and little by little, force it open until ties are eventually severed. This may be tempting if you don't like his family. But it's not healthy, or fair to him, and he in turn shouldn't do this to you either. Because one day the resentment may backfire. Conjure up the classy broad you have inside of you, remember that every family is different, and do what you can to tolerate them and support your husband. If you play nice and deal with them, he will, too, and he'll respect you even more for it in the long run.

Just remember, no matter what your situation, if you lay down the law from the beginning *in a calm but stern manner*, they will at least know where you stand from early on. Don't freak out, and don't just sit there and let anyone walk all over you, either, because again, this is the rest of your life – and you will be the one who suffers. If a particularly bad situation arises, wait until you cool down, calmly talk to your husband about it, and figure out what *you* need to do to deal with it in the most efficient way possible.

As we know, sometimes relationships can be severely unhealthy and even downright dangerous. But for many of us, the relationships we share with in-laws and family members are not this severe in scale; instead, they can be difficult and intrusive, and can screw with our well-being. It may be tempting to cut people off completely, but instead we should limit our interactions with said family members to keep them from negatively influencing our mental state. It doesn't mean never seeing them, or cutting them off. It just means deciding how much you are going to allow yourself to be bothered by them. I call it "weeding."

Get Your Hands in the Dirt

Sometimes it's so easy to pay attention only to what we can see or touch, and we don't realize the power of things that aren't in plain sight, like our thoughts. Since we can't literally "see" them, we can forget how much they affect us on a daily basis. The solution? Learn to garden. I'm not talking about hands-in-the-dirt, grow-your-own-veggies type of gardening (although that's great if you have an actual garden). You don't literally have to garden to have an idea of what it takes to maintain one. But all of us absolutely need to become *mental* gardeners.

Think about this for a moment: if you had a vegetable garden, small or large, you'd plant what you want to eat. You'd water your garden, watch it grow, and invest into it your precious time and energy - just as we do with our goals or intentions. But no matter how many layers of protection you have under the surface, it is inevitable that weeds will find their way in. You'll see them, a few at a time, popping up through the dirt. The problem is that those weeds eat up energy, so now those precious nutrients and energy that would be going to your veggies is being stolen and sucked up by those weeds. A good gardener knows they must stay on top of their garden and get rid of those weeds right when they sprout, so they can maintain healthy plants. The weeds bring nothing to the table (literally), and will only cause trouble.

It's up to you to do something about the weeds. If you ignore them or pretend they're not there, eventually they'll overrun your whole garden and kill your plants. If you just sit there and worry about them you won't be helping your garden, and you will only watch them choke out your healthy veggies that you want. Instead, you actually have to get your hands in the dirt and pull them out if you want to see results. Even though it may be a little annoying, you'll find when you get going that it's much easier than it looks. Once you are up close and tug on them, you'll see that the roots of the weeds are flimsy and pull right out. If you wait too long, those weeds can develop some pretty thick roots - you can still pull them out, you'll just need to work a bit harder at it.

Become a mental gardener. Pluck the weeds out, and watch the other things in your life thrive as the energy is free to flow where it should. Bad thoughts in your head are weeds, as are bad friends, bad habits, bad energy, and worries that hold no weight. The faster you learn how to pull those, the more energy you'll have for the good things in life. This may cause you to hesitate, and worry that this is selfish, but it's 100% the opposite. When you take care of your mental garden, you are allowing yourself to be the best version of YOU that you can be. This is the side of you that the world needs most.

Take a moment to assess some things:

o   What's a goal you have that you've been putting off?
o   What's been on your mind that you know you haven't given as much attention to as you'd like?
o   List the 3 most important things to you and your spouse for your wedding.

Pay attention to the following:

o   Negative thoughts that run through your head throughout the day.
o   Small things that eat up your time (mindless "errands", Facebook, web-surfing, etc.)
o   When your mind goes on "autopilot" (what are you thinking about? Is it healthy?)

Now ask yourself:

o   Which things are completely *necessary* for you to do, and which are not?
o   Are there any things/people that have been zapping your time or energy? (This could be anything from bad habits to one-way friendships.) Identify them as weeds. You know what to do.
o   Did you discover you're wasting time worrying about something that you can't do anything about?

I hope this inspires you to go grab a shovel. And, while we are on the topic of gardening, let's learn about our mother-in-laws through culinary herbs…

How your mother-in-law and others in your life can help you learn about herbs.

If you've never gardened before, a great place to start is by planting some herbs. In order to help us learn about herbs, let's describe them in terms of mother-in-laws.

Rosemary: The Antisocial MIL. Rosemary needs her space. Don't keep her with the rest of the herbs, because she doesn't need as much attention and in fact prefers to be neglected every so often (she is a glutton for punishment). She doesn't need to be fussed over, and she's pretty easy-going; she can stay outside in the ground, even during winter. You can use her fresh or dry her out, and she adds instant flavor to any dish. Just maintain your relationship with Rosemary, because if you don't, she can turn into a hot mess.

Thyme: Your BFF MIL. You'll want to keep thyme around for every season of your life. She's a great complement in winter comfort foods, but she's also great in marinades for a summer barbeque. She lays low and con-trolled, never invasive, and gets along great as a ground cover. You can call on her at any time and borrow her leaves whenever you need them.

Mint: The Overbearing Mother-in-Law. Be very, very careful with mint. She looks great, smells great, and you can enjoy a strong mojito with her. But good lord, if you let her in just a smidge, pretty soon she's overtak-ing all your space, and no matter how much you try to cut her back, the damage is done. Her roots are thick and know no boundaries, and she'll choke you out. She's lovely to have around – sometimes. You just need to keep her contained. Save her for a pot on your patio, and thank me later.

Sage: The Hippie MIL. Sage is a woody kind of herb. She's strong but mellow. If you love her flavor, plant her in the ground and let her grow big, although planting her in a container and cutting her back more regularly would control her a bit. If she gets too big, take some cuttings and share them with other yogi friends who can make "smudge sticks" out of them – bundles of sage and other herbs that "cleanse" an area when burned.

Tarragon: The Surprisingly Social MIL. Upon first meeting tarragon, if you are growing her from seed, you may think she's dead. No matter how much you poke and prod, you are left with one-word answers and no signs of life. But lo and behold, after a little time passes and a bit of nurturing, suddenly she springs to life and adds great flavor to your world. Don't give up on her; give her a chance and get to know her.

Cilantro: the Flighty, Freeloading MIL. Smells great, super-easy, and always ready for a party. Cilantro loves being thrown into a simple guacamole or fajita dish and adds instant flavor to any fiesta. The down-side is that she bolts pretty quickly and is pretty sporadic on coming back.

Basil: Your Favorite Ethnic MIL. Basil is an herb that you'll want in your garden no matter what your palette may be. She's always avail-able to you, very easy to harvest, and her seeds tend to spread and grow all around her. She's great in a simple tomato sauce, she smells fabulous, and she gets along with everyone – salads, pesto, pizzas and dressings. Who cares if you can't understand her half the time? She even gets along with other nationalities; Thai basil is a cousin that goes great in Asian dishes.

What type of herb is your mother-in-law? Go out and buy her a plant to match her personality. Cook her up a meal or serve her a drink with these herbs as a gesture of peace. But whatever you do, for God's sake, remember to keep the mint in the pot.

More on Family: Father of the Bride

Everyone knows that aside from your intimate first dance with your husband, your cake cutting, and your drunken cousin dancing on top of a speaker, one of the most prominent moments of your wedding night is when you take the stage with your father for the "father-daughter dance."

This can be a wonderful thing – if you have a great relationship with your father. I am lucky enough to say that I do, and I looked forward to this wonderful part of the evening. But I found during my polling that for some women, this part of the evening hits a nerve. They brought up an interesting point: What if your relationship with your dad is non-existent? Perhaps you loved your father, but he is sadly deceased. Or perhaps he exists on this earth, yet was not always "Dad of the Year," or did not have a large part in raising you. Or perhaps you don't know if he exists on this planet any longer, but if he does you ~~wish he would get run over by a truck~~ wish him well.

There are all sorts of situations, but perhaps Lauren describes her feelings best:

It should be said first that I'm not a big believer in marriage. There are a multitude of reasons for this; some based in cold hard facts, some based on personal flights of fancy. Regardless I do believe in weddings. I love them. There something so great about a big party that's supposed to celebrate two people in love and wanting to share that love with their nearest and dearest. Of course there is also tons of food and booze, usually a constant loop of decent music and lots of people having a fun-filled evening together. Everyone looks their best – men in suits and ties, ladies in cocktail dresses. The happy couple is all aglow. For most of the night, it's all magic.

But then the DJ or singer of the band breaks in to introduce the bride (again) and this time, her father. They take to the center of the dance floor and soon the opening bars of a painfully sappy song about butterfly kisses and loving her first and how unforgettable she is begins to play. This is also usually the moment I stand transfixed to my place. Despite myself and the utter rage and tragic longing that is overcoming me I can't look away. It's the epitome of the "car crash" saying – I know I should look away, excuse myself to the bathroom, or more appropriately the bar, but I can't move.

Please don't misunderstand. I don't begrudge the bride and her father this special moment. But I do feel it's a little insensitive. I've done some informal polling on the topic. As in, while standing there I look to my left and my right and count every third female has some sort of daddy-issues. I recently posted something on my Facebook wall to this same effect and several people "liked" it. This pained feeling that surrounds me at this portion of the evening is not a foreign concept. There are other girls out there that feel the same way. We all have the same look of wistfulness and nostalgia disguised as happiness for this good friend or family member as her daddy spins her around. At this moment I do not want to be angry with the bride, but it is hard not to be peeved when my perfectly enjoyable evening has turned to navel gazing as I sort through my own issues of abandonment and loss.

I'm not sure what the alternative is. If modern weddings are bucking tradition in other ways, why not this way, too? I've been to weddings recently where we toasted the couple with Amstel Light instead of champagne. If the bride's mother can walk her down the aisle and men can be "maids" of honor, why not skip the father-daughter dance? Maybe a jaunty family dance to something more uplifting – there are dozens of versions of Sister Sledge's "We Are Family". This is a joyous occasion, keep it light. However, if you insist on dancing with daddy, may I suggest something silly – a choreographed dance party to Will Smith's "Just the Two of Us", maybe? Or of course you can just make sure the bar is stocked with extra tequila and champagne for the rest of us.

Lauren offers an interesting alternative, in that we don't have to participate in this ritual. The beauty of wedding planning, especially in today's world, is that there really are no set rules. However, I do not feel that brides should forego a ritual that means something to them because of any guest who is attending.

For example, let's say you have a relative who just went through a horrible and painful divorce. You are sensitive to the fact that they are going through a tough time. But does that mean you should forego the first dance with your husband as to not upset said relative? Of course not. Because let's face it: you can put 250 people in a room, and 249 of them are going to have either an issue or an opinion (the 250th will be too drunk to notice.) Sure, you can try to do your best to accommodate everyone's needs. You can also stand twenty feet from a wall, run straight at it headfirst, and repeat this process until you bust through the sheetrock. The end result will be the same. But Lauren makes an excellent point: think about if it's important to you. If not, toss the idea and do something different.

I am not suggesting that you deliberately do something to hurt another's feelings. Just because you are a bride does not give you a free pass to disregard others or use your wedding to throw jabs in an effort to hurt anyone, of course. I think the key here, as a bride, is to stay true to your own life and to have your wedding reflect your own particular set of circumstances – not to feel pressured into an uncomfortable or forced situation for the sake of "tradition." But, given all the emotions that weddings can conjure up in all who attend, take Lauren's advice: No matter what you do, keep the bar stocked.

Back to the Dais

We've mingled with enough tables at this point, and now it's time to head back to the dais for a moment and talk about situations that can come up in our relationship.

It is inevitable in any intimate relationship that each individual will take on certain roles when living together. And by "roles", I do not mean "schoolgirl" and "naughty teacher" (although, hey, if those are your roles, more power to you). What I am talking about are certain responsibilities or chores that require our attention in our day-to-day lives, such as cooking, cleaning, handiwork and other household responsibilities.

When we first adjust to any new living situation, the roles we take on sometimes happen naturally. You likely have experienced this at certain other points in your life, such as living with a roommate (one always leaves a mess, the other is always stuck cleaning up after them), living in close quarters with a sibling, or even while going on vacation with a good friend. But these periods in our lives are usually not permanent – we will maybe one day get a place of our own, we will not live with our siblings forever, and the vacation will end.

Marriage, on the other hand, is a lifelong commitment. And if that commitment involves constantly picking up after someone else or doing a chore for which you never receive any help, there will inevitably be issues that take root.

When one person "owns" a certain role, the other will sometimes dismiss that role in their minds knowing that the other one will take care of it. In essence, they don't think about it anymore because they know that their partner will get it done. For instance, if you are always preparing dinner, then your husband will certainly expect after a while that this is your "role." If you enjoy cooking often, this may not be a big deal. But if you find yourself muttering under your breath and slamming pots and pans around at 6:30 after a long day while hubsivus is waiting around for you to put a hot plate on the table, problems can arise. If the scale is tipped too far to one side, resentment can creep in, and that's when the fighting starts.

You can fix this. But you need to step out of the situation and see it from another angle. If you are always taking charge and getting certain things done, you will probably see that *he is learning from you that he is excused from doing them.* The more time passes, the worse it can get.

Take it from Sherri Mills, author of the book *I Almost Divorced My Husband But I Went on Strike Instead.* According to Mills: "When I first got married, I didn't mind being the one to clean and cook. But once we had two kids, I needed help. I'd ask my husband, Gerald, to do the dishes or fold the laundry, and he would say yes but would never do it. The resentment got worse every year. Finally, I snapped. I was fixing dinner, and I asked our two kids, then 11 and 12, to run down the street and pick up an ingredient. They came back empty-handed. I was angry, but Gerald defended them. That was it. I announced, 'Not only am I not cooking dinner, but I am officially on strike.'"

Mills goes on to explain how she thought about divorce (yes, the resentment became that bad), but she didn't want to put her family through that. Instead, she drew up a contract detailing her one-year strike. She outlined seventy household chores that fell on her shoulders and stated that her husband needed to take responsibility for thirty-five of them. Until then, she would do *zero* of them. Her husband first became pompous and took on an "I'll show you" attitude, acting as though he could do it all with no problem. This lasted three days. He then tried to rebel, but she wasn't having it – she stuck to her guns. He had no choice but to do the laundry/cooking/clean-up while she sat on the couch. After two weeks, he came to her with a newfound respect – and an agreement to take on half the chores.

Ironically, her strike not only fixed the problem – it significantly improved their relationship: "He gained a new respect for me, and now I have a husband I don't resent. Gerald never went back to his old ways — I'll come home from work and he'll be shining the floors or ironing. I can't believe he's the same man I married! I read that people who share chores have better sex — and we're proof: Our sex life is hotter than ever." Hmph.

But as a key factor, she also goes on to admit that she was part of the problem. "I used to blame Gerald, but truthfully, I should never have allowed things to get so bad. My original contract called for a 50-50 division of chores, but I know that it won't be that way all the time. It doesn't really matter who does what, as long as both people are working toward the same goal."

You don't have to let things get as drastic as it did with the Mills family. Instead, learn from their situation. When you or your husband feel the scale being tipped too far in one direction, talk it out and work together to get it balanced again. If Sherri wasn't so determined to fix her marriage, and savvy as to how she went about it, her family may have been broken as a result.

One of the therapists I interviewed (who has asked to remain anonymous) discusses a similar situation in her marriage as well. She admits that every seven years, she and her husband would hit a rough patch. The most recent one was mainly due to the fact that she was always picking up after him, and he never helped out around the house. She goes on to explain how these things seem so minor, but they can really wear on your relationship little by little until you reach a breaking point – you lose respect for your spouse, and you really do wind up resenting them.

She confronted her husband and explained that she needed help. It was too much for her, and it was having a negative impact on their relationship. She explains, "I loved him, but I'm not going to do all the house work and then work full time. That's not the way it works…I'm not going to be a bitter old woman." She couldn't stay in the relationship and continue to feel this way.

But he did not want to help her. So they agreed to separate. They were going to wait a few months until their son's birthday passed, as they did not want him to go through a difficult time at that point, and they'd work out the details soon after. But when that time came, her husband approached her one day and said, "Where are we going on vacation this year?"

She looked at him for a moment, dumbfounded, and said, "Have you decided you're going to help out?"

He shook his head and said, "I guess so."

He did start doing some chores around the house, but eventually, they got a cleaning lady. "It was cheaper than a lawyer!" she laughs.

Good point. We have to do what works for our unique situations. And sometimes, a cleaning lady is a better investment than a lawyer and a therapist combined.

Examples from my own parents

My parents probably don't realize the positive influence they had on my life and relationships, just by setting great examples. Take, for instance, the way they used to fight.

I remember a particularly rough car ride home when I was about fifteen years old. My mom was insanely pissed about something my dad did. After listening to her complaining for a half-hour about how angry she was, I said, "Why don't you guys just get a divorce?"

She looked at me like I had twelve heads. In her thick New York accent, she firmly stated: "Whatta you, nuts? I was brought up Catholic." Oh, that's right! I totally forgot that it was unacceptable for anyone who is Catholic to get a divorce. What would the family think? To the more old-school types in many a Catholic family, divorces were reserved only for gay Uncle Jordan after he came out of the closet, and he didn't count because he was of course a godless sinner. But in all seriousness, and religion aside, my parents' determination to work through the tough times and stay together no matter what is the reason why they just celebrated their fortieth wedding anniversary, and I think we can all learn something from this example.

Regardless of the expected ups and downs, my parents had (and still have) a very give-and-take relationship that works for them, and when it comes to traditional roles of husband and wife, they certainly broke the mold. For example, my dad is terrified of bugs, so my mom is always the one we'd call if there were a spider in our bedroom. I once called my dad in, shrieking as I stood on the bed to get away from the spider on the wall. "Quick!!! It's gonna run again!" I shoved a tissue at my dad. He reluctantly took it, and then thirty minutes later when he got close enough to the thing, he pretended he couldn't reach it to kill it (the spider was at chest level).

Another time, when he found a centipede in the bathtub, he simply placed a cup over it so it couldn't get away and waited for my mom to come home to perform the execution. "Eh, Jo Ann, there's a *centerpiece* in the bathroom." (Did I mention he fucks up words?)

Of course, that's neither here nor there. The bottom line is that the non-traditional roles work for them in their marriage, as they may in our own marriage as well. So be open-minded (because every relationship is different), and always tune into keeping your marital scales balanced. Now, onto table #5…

Table #5: Haters

So you're engaged! You get to wear a white dress, and throw a big party to celebrate your happily ever after with the person of your dreams! And have your picture taken! And be a rock star for a day, surrounded by attention and people you love! Well then, guess what? *Cue the haters!*

Here they come, riding in on their jealousy-fueled hate train, chug-chugging that haterade. (And you can tell that shit is lemon-flavored based on their sour pusses.) *Choo chooooooooo!!!*

It's unfortunate, but haters do exist, and it's no surprise that they tend to rear their heads when someone they know becomes a bride.

There are two things brides should immediately learn about haters: 1) they are often narcissists, and 2) you can learn effective tactics on how to deal with them and keep their negativity out of your wedding (and your life). Let's first touch on narcissism:

Clinical definition: **Narcissism** *is the personality trait of egotism, vanity, conceit, or simple selfishness. Applied to a social group, it is sometimes used to denote elitism or an indifference to the plight of others.*

Throughout your wedding planning, you will hopefully be surrounded by people who love you, care about you, and want what's best for you. You'll all dance on clouds while choosing wedding entertainment, paint rainbows as you design your invitations, and ride together to shop for your bridal gown in an environmentally-friendly bus fueled by unicorn farts.

But unfortunately, as you get on with your planning, you may find that not *everyone* has what's best for you in mind. Sadly, some see your wedding as competition, and/or an opportunity to pull their narcissistic punches (see cRzybTch1 and accompanying strains).

Narcissists come in the form of both men and women, but for the sake of this book, let's refer to this character as "Narcy Darcy." It's hard to not let the Narcy Darcys bother you, but remember: every moment you spend getting annoyed or being upset over something someone else has done or said is a precious moment being taken away from your wedding, your life and your happiness. Even if you think you don't care, other people's negative energy has a funny way of permeating our worlds. So, how do we deal?

Martha Beck, writer and contributor to *O Magazine*, perfectly describes dealing with a narcissist as a game of tug-of-war, where the narcissist pulls on one end of the rope, and you pull the other trying to defend yourself or change them. Don't bother. Drop the rope. The next time they go to pull, there will be no one there, and they will fall flat on their narcissistic face.

During my wedding planning, I had a particular problem with someone in my circle. This person was making things difficult, going out of her way to be rude, being very selfish, and as a result, making me feel like shit on a chocolate fondue stick. She was doing everything in her power to have a bad time, on purpose, and making it very obvious she'd rather be anywhere else other than at a happy event for me. The behavior led right up to my wedding day where this Narcy Darcy displayed a shit-storm of negativity and lack of class. This, I should mention, is someone who I once believed I was very close to, yet who began acting very strange just as soon as I had a ring on my finger. I guess the wedding was the breaking point, and it was my harsh reality that some people just can't put their childish ways aside for another - not even on the most impor-tant day of their lives.

Several people noticed, and she made herself look like an idiot. But even in my happy state of mind, it was hard not to let her disrespectful and negative behavior get to me. At the hall, my husband and I were in our bridal suite all alone, waiting to be announced into the reception. My new mother-in-law popped her head in to wish us well, and could see that something was bothering me. I said I was fine, but she pressed until I gave in and told her.

Then, something magical happened.

Right in that bridal suite, standing there in my wedding dress, hold-ing the hand of her son, she gave me the most profound advice I have ever received. Advice that was so powerful it changed my mood right around. She put her hands on my shoulders, looked me dead in the eyes, and said: "FUCK. HER."

She then smiled lovingly, wished us good luck, and was on her merry way. Suddenly the clouds cleared and the weight was lifted, all thanks to this lovely and much-needed bitch-slap from my MIL. Who woulda thought?

Now, it's important to understand the concept of "FUCK. HER." It doesn't mean that you get angry, or hold any animosity toward Narcy Darcy (even though we all know how much she'd love the extra attention). It does not grant you permission to retaliate against her. It does not mean that you waste your precious time and energy trying to figure out what her problem is. You shouldn't give a slice of your three-tiered wedding cake about anyone who tries to bring you down on one of the best days of your life, in my opinion.

What it means is that you simply let it go. Save your energy, don't play the game, and move on with your life without harboring any negativity. It's a difficult task, but it can be done. This has become my mantra for when I am feeling upset over someone else's actions, and it works like a charm every time. "*Keep calm and carry on.*" "*FUCK. HER.*" Tomato, tomahto.

As I always say to my sister when dealing with a Narcy Darcy: "Let them have it." Whatever they feel they need from you – whether it's to compete with you, bully you, to feel like they have "one-up'd" you, to be "better" than you or *whatever* – just ignore them and let them think they've won. Don't waste a drop of energy feeding into their antics. The less attention to pay to negative people, the better; they'll eventually move on to another target, and you will fly under their radar as if you never existed. It's a much better option than grabbing them by the ankle and flinging them off the nearest bridge (as tempting as that may be).

Not sure if you're dealing with a Narcy? Martha Beck gives us some helpful hints:

> "Think of someone in your life who seems to have an abundance of self-satisfaction. Now think about the way you feel after an interaction with this person. If you feel warm, nourished and valued, you've probably encountered someone with healthy self-esteem. But if the conversation leaves you feeling ashamed, confused, self-doubting or invisible, break out the red flags. It's highly likely you're dealing with a narcissist."

In short, identify the Narcy, use these tools to deal with them, and when applicable, run like hell from these emotion-sucking troublemakers.

And remember: it's not really you they are in competition with, anyway. It's their sad selves.

Open Letters to the Narcy Darcy's in Our Life

Everyone has their own story, usually hysterical, of what they wish they could say to this one person if they didn't need to worry about family politics or sabotaging lifelong friendships.

Here are a few letters from anonymous individuals to the N.D. in their lives, saying what they really mean, without ruining every Thanksgiving from here on in. Weddings are supposedly the most "wonderful time in our lives," for the bride and groom, but these lovelies had a funny way of making things all about them.

Dear Bridesmaid,

You're a pain in the ass. I don't care what you say, you are going to walk with the short, fat, dumpy bald guy because you're short too! Its not your wedding, and it's height order, so stop bitching!

Love the bride

~~~~~~

Dear Guest,

You are one of my closest friends, and you coming to our wedding and being a part of our day meant so much. We love that you enjoyed yourself at our reception and we're pretty certain that everyone noticed. We never expected that the professional band we hired as entertainment wouldn't be the sole entertainment at our wedding reception.

Sure, we know you love to dance, and of course, we've danced alongside of you in clubs and bars on our many nights out enjoying the town. We just didn't expect our wedding guests to be treated to dance moves reminiscent of a burlesque show present at a gentleman's club.

At times you were the only person dancing out there in front of my 105 yr. old great grandmother, my aunts, uncles, and other God-fearing relatives. We would look around the room and see 75 yr. old women with their jaws dropping, completely unable to look away from moves they've never seen outside of a scantily clad woman in an old Russ Meyer movie. Their blushing husbands all huddled together, sheepishly chuckling amongst themselves.

Even your own husband couldn't stop you. You just kept on without a care in the world. I can't tell you how many of my uncles and cousins approached my dad, asking if he thought you would accept singles. My own mom even asked, "Who is the stripper you invited?"

We were horrified, yet just nervously laughed when we noticed children innocently dancing beside you. They were trying to imitate your moves, looking up to you as if you were an angel sent from heaven - in this case, stripper heaven. Their moms were overcome with horror at the ghastly spectacle.

Bless your heart, you were the TALK of our wedding and we even have you or parts of you in every single professional photo in our wedding album. You know, a limb here and there, and a stray arm or leg protruding out from behind the beautiful profile of me and my new husband dancing to our wedding dance song.

To THIS DAY, when our wedding is mentioned, YOU are what people talk about.

While we're happy you had an outlet to practice your erotic dancing skills - please, for future receptions you attend, at least offer the Bride and Groom 20% of your tips.

Still your friend,

The Bride

Dear Mother-in-law,

I love you, I really do, and I think it's great that I feel this way about you since most women don't really like their mother-in-laws. And yes, perhaps I am a bit on edge due to the stress that a wedding can bring to a bride-to-be, and the irritability level is super high right now. But really, the last thing I need is for you to start "reminding" me to send thank you cards from my shower - which took place just a week and a half ago. When you brought this up to me as if I needed you to explain it to me, I was taken aback. The gall! My heart began to race with thoughts of people talking about the fact that they had not yet received a 'thank you' one week later, as I was rushing to get them out, while still taking the effort to write more than the robotic, "thank you for the..." Are people actually sitting around waiting for them?! Ugh! While I understand you want to make sure people are properly thanked for their gifts, I can assure you that I am on it. I am efficient, thankful, and my mother taught me proper etiquette. The card will be in the mail shortly. So please, stop stressing me out, back off just a bit, and give a girl a chance.

Sincerely,
The Bride

Table #6: Ceremony

The ceremony is the single most important part of your wedding, since it is here that you officially become husband and wife. Because of this, make sure you spend your time on details and have it personally reflect you and your groom. Since we all have different traditions, beliefs, faith and family, there are no set rules as to how to plan your ceremony, but the best thing is to have it honor both you and your husband. (Or wife, or donkey. Just trying to be PC here.)

For those of us marrying someone of the same religion, the ceremony can be a breeze to plan since you know what is expected. If, on the other hand, you are marrying someone of different religious faith and traditions, be careful not to offend anyone and to do your best to honor both sides. It doesn't matter how much or little you believe in your spouse's family's traditions, you still need to find some common ground and compromise. If you can't do that at this point, you are setting yourself up for a very tough time doing so at any other point in your marriage, and this in turn could foreshadow a marriage full of conflicting opinions ranging from how to raise your kids to how to prepare your vegetables.

Planning a wedding is a good exercise in practicing respectful give-and-take, with your own family as well as your spouse's. (Like it or not, they are now your family as well.) If you can't come up with a healthy compromise, maybe forego both and explore the option of having your own ceremony based on traditions that mean something to the two of you.

If you fall in love with a specific location, remember that those who are in charge there will have their own set of rules. Start by asking what sorts of requirements they have for marrying on their grounds. If it's a particular church you have fallen in love with, see what getting married there entails, and be prepared to be asked to join their congregation first. Just remember: While American weddings are mostly all about the reception site, don't book anything until you are sure you can book your ceremony for the same date.

For many brides and grooms, the officiant is the most important part of their ceremony. I will vouch for this first-hand by letting you in on my sister's experience.

My sister and brother-in-law's ceremony was amazing. She did her homework and chose an officiant who provided a personal, warm and perfectly-timed ceremony. It was touching, while provoking a few light-hearted laughs, too. The result was an intimate marriage ceremony that still somehow allowed everyone in the church to feel like we were all a part of their big day. As an added bonus, no one fell asleep or passed out. The church they chose was beautiful, but they honestly could have married almost anywhere – it was the officiant who made the ceremony. In my sister's words:

"I spent a lot of sleepless nights over this one in the engagement phase. I cannot tell you how many late night conversations took place that left me stressed and just wanting to run away and elope!

I am Catholic, and my now-husband is not. He was actually not raised with any faith. (Which, to some people, of course means he is the spawn of Satan.)

The one stipulation that my hubby had from before we even got engaged was that he did not want a Catholic ceremony, and I agreed. Like I said, I was raised Catholic, but am by no means a Charlie church-goer, or a poser that pretends to be, and I always wanted a personalized ceremony that reflected us as a couple. Not what the Bible said it should be. It wasn't an option to have the ceremony at the catering hall, which would have been the obvious choice, and I won't get into why we couldn't.

Well, my mother kept beating this into me: "Your grandmother will be devastated! You must get married in the church!" But this was one of the few things my husband asked me for in terms of the wedding, and I needed to compromise. In the words of my husband: "Sorry Granny." (He loves Granny, by the way).

I decided to go on a six-month long expedition that was exhausting, to find a "non-denominational" church that would allow me to bring in my own pastor to marry us. I finally found a church, and it was beautiful. I was met with such opposition by my mother…after all, what would people think? But I stuck to my guns on this one. Granny didn't notice, and to this day, people still comment on how wonderful our ceremony was. It was honestly my favorite part of the whole day. It was all of 10 minutes, and truly showed who WE are as a couple.

Bottom line: Stay true to yourself and your husband, and it will work out in the end! Don't get so caught up in what Grandma wants, or what 'Aunt Betsy' will say, or whoever…it is YOUR DAY, DO IT YOUR WAY!!"

When determining your ceremony site and/or officiant, here are some important things to consider:

- Check out the site in person. The only exception here is if you are planning a destination wedding. Otherwise, get your sexy little ass out there and see what's what.
- Meet with your officiant in person, if possible. Nowadays it's so incredibly easy for anyone to become an officiant that it's actually kind of scary. Doing everything online and filling out questionnaires does not make up for a face-to-face meeting with another

human being – especially one who will be responsible for one of the most important ceremonies of your life. They may look great on paper, but when Joey Tribiani shows up at the altar on your wedding day, don't say I didn't warn you.

- Inquire about ceremony music. Do you need to bring in a musician, or will they provide music?
- Inquire about any necessary religious documents.

When planning your ceremony, you also may want to consider if you'll have a receiving line. This is where, after the ceremony, the bride and groom will wait at the exit of the church or ceremony site so they can greet everyone as they leave. This is really your choice. Some couples opt-out of the receiving line, and instead, have everyone line up outside with bubbles, beach balls, rose petals or what-have-you so they can run through for a nice photo-op before being whisked away to the reception. That's fine, too. My advice is that you just be sure you choose one of three times to connect with everyone at your wedding:

- at the church,
- during your cocktail hour, or
- at the beginning of the reception.

Some couples opt to be absent from their cocktail hour so they can make a grand entrance into the reception. Others decide to go to their cocktail hour so they get the formal "hellos" out of the way before the reception. If I could go back and do it again, I would skip the receiving line at the church, and go to my cocktail hour to say hello to everyone, rather than waiting to be announced into the reception. My husband and I had a great time at our wedding, but we spent the first quarter of the reception making rounds to say hello, and missed out on some prime dancing.

If you opt out of the receiving line and decide to run out of the church, be leery about having people throw things at you or blow bubbles in your face. No matter how much brides think this would be a great idea, they almost always forget that they are *giving people something to throw at them*, which results in photos full of squinted-eyes and hands up, blocking what is coming at them. One brave couple I know had little custom beach balls handed out at the church. Great idea, but they opened themselves up to a Billy Madison-style dodgeball session as they made their elegant exit. While this couple in particular made it out unscathed, it was still a risky move – especially if your hubby's frat brothers will be in attendance.

Rehearse

No matter what type of ceremony you choose, remember to have a rehearsal. The process may seem simple enough to you and your wedding party, but factor in nerves, stage fright and the plenty of little things you overlook, and suddenly you become the deer in headlights. Better safe than sorry.

Based on some polling, here are some common "loves" and "loathes" people had when discussing wedding ceremonies:

Ceremony loves: Short, sweet vows; flower girls and ring bearers; classy music; a warm and engaging officiant; a cozy, intimate atmosphere; a guestbook that will be a keepsake for you and your partner; a few well-placed rituals, such as a unity candle, blending of sand, drinking of wine or breaking the glass.

Ceremony loathes: Over-personal, inside-joke vows that make the audience feel like they are spying on you in your bedroom; a forty-two person bridal party brigade; an officiant who reprimands the audience or couple instead of celebrates; programs, which are not only wasteful in production, but will mostly be thrown out the moment the guests leave the church; a slew of rituals that go on longer than a marriage.

Last but not least, don't forget to write a "thank you" note to the person who marries you. Maybe you were already planning on doing so, but it's surprising how many people accidentally overlook this. Considering new brides are working off of a list of guests who have given gifts when writing their cards, it can be easy to forget. We wrote a "thank you" card to the priest who married us, and a few weeks later we received a card from him thanking us for the "thank you" - along with a blessing. We thought that was great. As for that extra blessing? Hey, every little bit helps.

Here is a little bit of my own experience on the day of our wedding: There I was, in the little room off to the side in the back of the church, waiting for everyone to be seated so I could walk down the aisle. My dad stuck his head in the room, and said…well, not much. He was pretty much scared shitless and could barely speak. But soon it was time, and I slipped my arm through his.

Right as the doors opened, and we were about to round the corner and come into view of everyone, the drivers of the limo noticed that my veil was caught on the beading of my dress and bunched up – in several places. They stopped me before I came into view so that they could fix it. It took so long that I actually heard the violinist and organist re-start the tune I was supposed to walk down the aisle to as the guests stood staring at an empty church doorway. Later, my mother-in-law told us that at that moment she thought to herself, "Tough luck, son, looks like she bailed." But alas, the guys managed to untangle my veil, and off we went. Why do I tell you this? Because shit. Will. Go. Wrong. You can't stress about it.

Just for fun: Some interesting (and somewhat nutty) pre-ceremony traditions from different parts of the world

"Blackening the Bride" (Scotland): This tradition takes place before the wedding. The bride (and possibly the groom as well) are snuck up on at some point in the days leading up to their wedding, and basically "slimed" with disgusting substances. "It can be curdled milk, rotten eggs, spoiled curry, smelly fish sauces, molasses, mud, flour, sausages, syrups and feathers," explain the folks over at cultureledger.com. And you thought that nasty leopard-print g-string all up in your grill from the guys at Hunk Mania was gross.

"Kidnapping the Bride" (Germany): Days before the wedding, it is customary that German brides are "kidnapped" by friends and family. The groom needs to "find" his bride, and the amount of love he has for her is determined by how quickly he can do so. The search begins at local pubs, where the groom stops to have a beer while collecting hints from local patrons. Good thing this doesn't happen in America – I'd surely be waiting a while, especially if Sam Adams Octoberfest is on tap. "At times the ritual ended badly," say the folks at cultureledger.com. No. Fucking. Way! Now there's a shocker!

"Clanging pots and pans," aka "Charivari" (France): According to Wikipedia, Charivari "is the term for a French folk custom in which the community gave a noisy, discordant mock serenade, also pounding on pots and pans, at the home of newlyweds. The community used noisemaking and parades to demonstrate disapproval." Sigh. If only it were that easy here in the States. Instead, people talk smack, make passive-aggressive comments, and offer uninvited opinions. The jury is still out as to which is louder.

"Nibbling a biscuit around a boy's neck" (Greece): This one just sounds creepy. Does this really happen? According to the website Environmental Graffiti, the answer is yes. "A young Greek bride ritually celebrates her nuptials by grabbing a young, prepubescent boy and forcing him onto her lap. Then, she bites the biscuit ring that surrounds his neck off and finally releases him from the neck nibbling." I didn't see it in "My Big Fat Greek Wedding," and that is the bible of truth for me. And wouldn't that be illegal? We brides wouldn't want to be accused of being a, as my dad says, "paraphernalia."

"Fattening the bride" (Mauritania): Ahaha. Hahahahahaha. I'd love to see this fly here. "Men on this side of the globe want women fat; the fatter, the better…the practice is called 'Leblouh,' and is mandated in these parts of the world so that women will be considered attractive to their future mates." I think I just heard all American brides shed five pounds due to the stress that reading these words induced.

"Not going to the bathroom" (Malaysia): In Malaysia, it is not permitted for the bride or groom to go to the bathroom for seventy-two hours before their "I do's." The practice is apparently taken so seriously that the couple is placed under surveillance during this time to ensure they don't cheat. "The belief is that if the couple survives this torture, they will not only have abundant fertility, but none of their children will die." And if they don't? Oh, right.

This isn't totally relevant here, but I peed on my friend in the bathroom on my wedding day. I didn't mean to, but she was helping me with my dress, and it just sort of happened. Don't judge me. You try locating a toilet under a circus tent of organza. You don't know who your real friends are until they are holding up twenty pounds of tooling without letting it hit the floor, and refrain from dropping it when you accidentally spritz them with a tinkle.

"Broken dishes," aka "Polterband" (Germany): This ritual is said to keep ghosts and poltergeists away from the bride and groom, and bring good luck. "Friends and family bring lots of dishes to the ceremony. They smash the dishes against bricks–the more dishes the better! Afterwards, the bride and groom have to clean up all the broken pieces. This ritual symbolizes breaking and removing their old lives and starting a new life together." Hmm. I thought this ritual was reserved for the first fight? Oh well – better the relatives' dishes than your new china.

"Spending way more money than you can afford on a four-hour event": America.

Back to the Dais: Are you there, God?

Now we go back to the dais to discuss a topic that may be important in your marriage: religion. Religion and spirituality are very personal, and each of us is of course entitled to our own beliefs. We all have our reasons, whether based on nature or nurture, which mold our belief systems and faith. I don't care if it's Allah, Buddha, Jesus, the man from kickboxing class – it doesn't matter. But I think it's helpful to believe in something, and to have a little faith. For all intents and purposes in this section, I am going to refer to whatever it is you believe in as "God". Your God may be a living being, a figurative being, an energy source - whatever. The point is, *you gotta believe.*

If you find yourself at a standstill with your faith, take a step back and re-evaluate. No matter how many times you go to church, if nothing resonates within you, maybe it's time to do some thinking. Try to choose something that makes you feel good and follow it, making it your own personal religion.

It can be Bikram yoga, which you make a pact to attend thrice weekly and endure the smelly farts of the person in front of you in an effort to conjure up your inner Zen. It can be cooking class, where you learn the process of turning just a few ingredients into a meal for yourself or a family in need. It can be having lunch with your grandmother once a week, where you will listen intently as she tells you stories of her youth, no matter if she can't remember a lick of what really happened and she makes you grilled cheese with her iron.

Just commit to something that fulfills you and makes you feel humble and connected, and makes your soul feel good. Not only will you feel good, but you'll want to help others feel good, as well.

Finding your God is important in life, but it can be extremely helpful around the time of your wedding. Many different churches and religions require some sort of pre-marriage counseling session that you must attend before your marriage ceremony. For me and my husband, since we were both raised Catholic, it was Pre Cana.

Either way, it seems that if we strip away the labels of religions and forget about the separate groups, we will see that many religions teach similar values in terms of marriage. I was able to see this firsthand with two therapists that I interviewed: a husband and wife team of Christian marriage counselors.

Meet Drs. Beverly and Tom Rodgers

"We want couples to learn that true love is less magic and more hard work than the media would like us to believe, that falling in love is different from staying in love, and that loving someone means wanting to heal the pain of their soul, as they in turn heal yours. True, soul healing love is possible." - Drs. Beverly and Tom Rodgers, authors of Soul Healing Love

I showed up at my meeting with Drs. Beverly and Tom Rodgers not knowing what to expect. Up until this point, I had been conducting my interviews one-on-one, and the idea of a husband and wife team intrigued me. It also scared the shit out of me, since they are Christian marriage counselors.

Although I was brought up Catholic, I did not want a biased opinion on marriage based on any particular religion. I wanted the information presented in this book to apply to *anyone* entering into marriage, and I wasn't sure if this would be the case with Tom and Bev.

As I walked into the restaurant to meet them, the questions swirled through my mind. Would I have to tip-toe around the vibe of my book? Would their information pertain to all brides and grooms, regardless of their religion?

Suddenly it hit me in that moment that I was about to walk into a meeting to ask two Christian marriage counselors to contribute to my book, called *THE REAL-DEAL BRIDAL BIBLE*. This may not go so well. What was I thinking? Shit. Shit! Could I even say *shit*?!

It was too late to turn back. I walked in, we shook hands, and I took my seat in the booth across from them. Luckily, their warm welcome and personable demeanors instantly put me at ease.

Speaking with Tom and Bev reminded me that no matter what (if any) religious group we are a part of, we are all under an even bigger umbrella: We are all *human*. And as humans, we take part in relationships. As it so happens, Tom and Bev are simply two humans who ran into trouble with their own marriage, and from their experiences emerged the passion and willingness to help others. In their book *Soul Healing Love,* they describe the despair in which they found themselves, which ultimately led them to their cause:

"We would do fine until one of us was triggered. The situation could be incidental. You may have similar circumstances in your own relationship. Things between you and your spouse start out benign, then, before you know it, you are in an all-out fight and you are not even sure what caused it. You try to tell yourself that you are overreacting. You may even tell yourself to calm down or even shut up, but to no avail. Your reaction triggers a reaction in your spouse, and now you are both deep in a power struggle.

"Without healthy communication tools, you feel stuck. You may be verbal, like Tom was in our early marriage, and yell and threaten, or you may simply pout and become icy like I did. But the results are still the same. You are distant and alone with no resolution in sight. We hated these times in the beginning of our relationship. We've even developed a name for them. We call them 'marital purgatory.'"

Tom and Bev will be the first to admit that simply being of a religious faith did not grant any exemption from the woes of marriage.

"We thought being strong Christians would immunize us against the hurt from our dysfunctional families of origin…Unfortunately, this did not happen.

"When you get engaged everything is fun, it's wonderful. We say they don't sit next to each other, they sit ON each other. Of course it's fantastic! You're sporting a diamond, you picked a place, you put down all your deposits. We do relationship counseling, and that's *before you even get engaged.* We thought, 'Nobody's going to take us up on this.' But people actually come to us and say, 'We want to get counseling to make sure this is smart for us.' We go over sex, money, roles, in-laws, child-rearing, religion, jealousy, time spent outside the marriage, all the hot topics that research shows couples split over. If you don't ask yourself those questions before you get engaged, you won't answer them honestly after you get engaged."

Whether the couple has been married for twenty years or is just now beginning to think about marriage, Tom and Bev encourage individuals to look deep within themselves and their past to understand their own patterns. This in turn helps them better understand their partner/spouse.

Almost always, they are met with resistance from one or both of the individuals when they propose this method, and rightfully so – it does seem a bit extreme at first to dig down into your own pasts when all you are trying to do is get on with your future as a couple. Why should you go back and experience pain from your childhood or past relationships? Their answer lies in the fact that in order to truly heal ourselves, we need to acknowledge that pain and make it work for us rather than against us. The more we run from it, the worse it gets. In their book, they cite the example of leprosy to better help us understand:

"Dr. Paul Brand, a physician who worked for many years with lepers, thinks that the greatest problem in treating leprosy is that the afflicted persons have lost their ability to sense and feel pain. Because of this, their tissue can actually deteriorate long before any pain signal is sent to the brain. Lepers are then in serious physical trouble before they are even aware of it. Without feeling the pain, they cannot effectively deal with their disease. For a leper, pain is truly a gift."

Overall, what I learned from Tom and Bev is that we all carry around our own forms of hurt and pain, and it is very likely that these feelings will creep up within our marriages. While not many people speak openly about this, it's normal, and most everyone deals with it on some level. The best way to have it work for you instead of against you is to acknowledge the issues rather than run from them.

Be the Buffalo

"The cow runs away from the storm while the buffalo charges directly toward it – and gets through it quicker." ~Wilma Mankiller, the first ever female chief of the Cherokee nation

Ever notice sometimes that the more you resist something, the worse it gets? Whether it's something you don't want to happen, an event you are dreading, a task you're avoiding, or something someone else is doing to upset you, it seems the more you try to avoid that very thing, the more it affects you. Certain things are out of our control. They just are what they are - and that's okay. Instead of resisting the storm, try the alternative – face it head on and roll with it. Be the buffalo. Because no matter how fast you can run, eventually the storm will catch up to you. I came across a poem which explains this concept beautifully…

Yet You Can
by Ralph Marston

You cannot succeed in fighting against the wind. Yet you can harness its power and do great things with it.
You cannot now be anywhere other than in this moment. Yet you can transform this very moment into whatever kind of experience you wish to live.
You cannot stop the sun from setting. Yet you can prepare yourself to make the very most of the new day that comes when the sun surely rises again.
You cannot stop the years from passing. Yet you can fill each one of those years with a life that's rich in meaning.
There are many things beyond your control. Yet you can live

true to your most authentic purpose no matter what may come.
You cannot be sure of what the future will bring. Yet you
can choose right now, and always, to continue bringing your
own unique beauty to life.

"Many of our fears are tissue-paper-thin, and a single courageous
step would carry us clear through them." -Brendan Francis

Table #7: Reception

Choosing your reception hall is the second most important part in planning your wedding, after choosing your ceremony details. The reception will likely cost the most money, and will involve the most details and coordination.

There are so many factors to check out when planning a reception that it's hard to think of everything, so hopefully this guide will help you think outside the box and consider all options. Remember, many places require a hefty deposit, and if you change your mind once you sign that contract you may not see that deposit ever again. So do your homework, follow these guidelines, and cover all bases before booking your place.

First, put on your business hat while looking for a reception hall. Remember, you will fall in love with certain places, you will imagine yourself having your first dance in the room, you will envision the centerpieces, and you will picture the dance floor filled with all of your guests. That part is easy and fun.

But going into your search with your business hat on will allow you to take a clear look at the not-so-obvious parts that you may not like. Maybe the place is gorgeous, but the bathrooms are horrible. Perhaps the service is great, but with a little digging you find that the food is not. These things are important, so scratch the surface and consider all angles.

"First came love and a baby carriage,
Hardly knew the people at my own damn marriage,
An open bar can open your mind..." ~ Train, "Half Moon Bay"

While searching for a hall, determine the number of guests you plan on inviting. There is no use checking out that intimate castle that holds fifty people when your mother has forty-two people already coming – and that's just from her nail salon. Figure out your golden number (remembering to compromise on both sides, of course). Keep in mind that certain places will tell you that their reception room will accommodate much more than it will comfortably fit. If your room is too small, you may all be on top of each other. Too large, and it will look and feel empty (and so will your dance floor).

As a side note: No matter what type of wedding you go for or what your particular style is, stay as true to yourself as you can. This will build up your immune system against cRzybTch1.

One of the most common threads I kept hearing when interviewing women from all different walks of life was that brides today have so much information to consider when it comes to their reception that it's hard to make the right decisions. Not only are we seeing what all of our friends are doing, but the circus freak show that is the media gives us views into lavish celebrity weddings as well. So while our parents had the weddings of friends and relatives to compare, we now have the Kardashians and Kendra Wilkinson setting the bar. It's unrealistic, and we may find ourselves veering off into a direction that really isn't our style. Stay focused, and try your best to tune everyone else out in order to plan a wedding that truly reflects you and your hubby's personalities and budgets.

Be a guest at your own wedding

Try to envision attending your wedding as a guest instead of as a bride. Remember, on your wedding day you will be pulled in a million different directions and the night will be a blur. Chances are you'll barely get a moment to eat. Because of this, you won't be able to experience the event fully and take in all the details as a guest would. Make sure you'd be comfortable if you came to your wedding.

Reception Hall Checklist

Use this checklist when assessing reception halls:

***Bathrooms** – Are they in good condition? Are they easily accessible (especially if you have many elderly guests, or guests with special needs)? Will you need to bring in baskets filled with hairspray, gum, etc., or do they provide any?

***Bridal Suite** – Is it large enough to accommodate your party? Will any food be served? (This is particularly important if you will not be attending your cocktail hour.)

***What vendors do you need to bring in**? For instance, does the hall provide the tables, chairs, linens? Or do you need to bring in your own suppliers? If so, who do they recommend?

***Does the hall require you to use certain vendors**? Some vendors strike deals with halls to ensure that all of their brides use them. Are you comfortable with these vendors? If not, don't be afraid to tell the hall you'd like to bring in your own. If you ask nicely before signing your contract, the hall will likely make an exception. I did this with a few of my vendors, and the hall agreed.

***How many entrée options** do they offer? Consider a vegetarian choice, and if they have alternatives for allergies (gluten-free, peanut-free, etc.)

***Will there be enough seats in your cocktail hour for everyone to sit down?** Because nothing is more difficult as a guest during a cocktail hour than having to juggle a drink, purse, shawl, tiny plate and fork, and place card while trying to ~~hit on the busboy~~ mingle with friends.

*Where will the cocktail hour be held? If you are planning to have an outdoor cocktail hour, be sure to ask where it will be held if it should happen to rain. Mother Nature can sometimes be a real Bitch.

Wherever you choose to hold your reception, don't be afraid to call and check in every once in a while to make sure things are on track. Don't overdo it, of course, but there's nothing wrong with an occasional phone call to ask questions or confirm details. Some women have no problem with this, and I think that is great. I, on the other hand, was always worried about "bothering" people, so I tended to be a bit more passive. But looking back, I fully support Meredith's advice:

"Be annoying. Stay on top of them. Do not always assume they have it under control. Nowadays, they try and get away with giving you as little as possible for as much money as they can. It is the sad truth, but with the economy the way that it is, they will try to cut corners. Get everything in writing, everything from time schedule to table linens! If it is not in your contract, they can and will try to get away with short-changing you."

Also, before you sign anything, check the cancelation policies with the hall and the county in which you are having your reception. This is not to say that you will call off your wedding, but sometimes the unforeseeable happens and a date needs to be changed or canceled. When it comes to protection, some counties favor the consumer while others favor the business. You don't want to be SOL if God forbid you need to change your date. Even if the contract says the hall will not refund your payments and/or deposit, the county laws may say otherwise, and you will have a case on your hands.

Types of Receptions

There are many types of receptions you can choose from. We are fortunate in that we live in a time where non-traditional is the norm, and anything goes. Between the internet and magazines, there's no excuse to not be creative, and especially while on a budget, you can still have a beautiful reception. I know plenty of brides who are afraid of appearing "tacky" if they choose to scale it back and have a more intimate event, but trust me - no matter what your budget is, it can be done. It's not the size of the event or the money you spend, but it's the execution and the details. So long as you keep your event personal and consider all of the important factors, you will be fine.

You could spend eighty grand on a beautiful fairy tale wedding and wear a tiara dripping with diamonds, but if you are serving cheese and crackers at your cocktail hour because you ran out of money after booking the fireworks extravaganza during your first dance, that's tacky. If you invite 400 people to the ritziest place in town for a Saturday night wedding and don't have an open bar for at least a short while during your event, that's tacky. If you run around telling everyone how your dress cost seven thousand dollars while they squabble over carrots and celery sticks, that's tacky. It's like the guy who drives a Mercedes and walks into the club wearing $500 shoes, but eats Ramen noodles and has nothing in his wallet but maxed-out credit cards. Don't be that guy. Be honest with yourself about your budget, and plan a beautiful wedding accordingly – and within your limits. That being said, let's go over a few reception options…

Cocktail Reception: This type of reception can be great for smaller weddings, or if you are on a tight budget. It also can be very fun and encouraging for partiers. It can still be elegant and semi-formal. Just be upfront in your invitation so that guests know what to expect. You don't want to lead guests to believe that it will be a traditional wedding with a sit-down dinner. *Positives*: The "cocktail" reception will be an uninterrupted party, since no one has to leave the dance floor at any particular time for dinner; you will save money, since this is more cost-effective than a formal sit-down meal. *Negatives*: Because no one is telling guests when to eat, you run the risk of people forgetting to do so and getting pretty shitfaced.

Brunch Reception: A brunch reception can be extremely elegant, and there are many reasons to consider this type of event. They usually consist of a lighter menu, a more manageable bar tab, and more affordable prices on just about everything else. *Positives*: You can save lots of money on vendors and the reception site; you can leave for the honeymoon later that day; you'll have less drinking, which means a reduced chance of Uncle Billy falling off the wagon and trying to hook up with one of your bridesmaids. *Negatives*: You won't have much time to spend getting ready since it's in the morning, and if you are a party person, having a low-key early wedding could be tough to come to terms with.

Saturday Evening Reception with Sit-Down Dinner: Ka-ching! Get ready to shell out the big bucks here. Most women want a Saturday night reception, because it usually sets the tone for a serious party. *Positives*: Your guests will be revved up, sexified, and ready to dance like no one's watching. *Negatives*: Get ready to lay down some beaucoup Benjis. Also, if you have a popular date in mind that falls on a Saturday (ie: 11/12/13, etc.), be prepared to snag the date early. It helps if you have a first-born already, and that you bring said child with you when booking the hall – they may ask for it along with your deposit.

Holiday Weekend Reception: Something else to think about is the weekend you choose to have your reception. Holiday weekends are often less expensive, since many people are on vacation. Take Susan's advice:

"We lived in a city far from our families, so all family was going to travel in for our wedding. We chose to have the wedding where we lived, instead of us traveling back to one of our home towns. We picked a three-day holiday weekend (Labor Day), to give our families a better opportunity for travel and time away from work. Because of this, we also delayed leaving for our honeymoon until the Tuesday after we got married and spent the long weekend with our friends and families. One of the best decisions we made!"

Backyard (or Park) Reception: There may be a time during your planning that you entertain the idea of a wedding reception in your parent's backyard, or at a local park. Maybe you are turned off by the cost of catering halls, or want a more "low-key" celebration. This can be an excellent choice, and if you or someone you know has a great yard and is willing, you may have your reception site. But as with all the others, weigh out your pros and cons. *Positives*: The celebration can be more intimate, and you can party all night long. You also aren't tied to any rules and can call all the shots on anything you want. *Negatives*: Surprisingly, this can become very expensive. You will need to bring in tables, chairs, food, flowers, and any other details. The weather may not cooperate, so you will need to think about a tent. And once it's over, whoever is hosting has a big mess on their hands. If it is a park you are looking at, they may have a noise ordinance that prevents you from having a deejay or band.

Destination Wedding: The idea of a destination wedding can be extremely appealing for certain couples, and for good reason. You get to experience new things, usually in an exotic and romantic location, you can make a vacation out of it for your guests, and often these ceremonies are very intimate. While some women do not have this option due to important family members who will not be able to travel, such as grandparents or parents, the ones who do may want to explore this option. Below are a few bits of advice from brides who have been through it:

"So my husband and I got married a bit later than most people do. We met when he was 36 and I was 31, and were engaged right before my 32nd birthday. We had both watched all of our friends and family get married and go through the crazy big wedding and all the theatrics that went along with it. I guess you can say that we learned a lot from others' trials and tribulations.

So when it became our turn, we decided to turn the tables a bit. I just could not see spending all that money on one night that goes way too fast. You are so busy trying to make sure you say hello and thank you to everyone that you lose that time to just enjoy the fact that it is your wedding day. So we decided that a destination wedding was in order. And not a crazy destination wedding where everyone is invited and you feel bad because people either can't come or have to spend tons of money to come. Instead we invited just the immediate family — our parents and siblings — to come down to Cancun with us for a week.

We had the most intimate, wonderful wedding on the beach with the people who mattered most. And not only that, but we got to spend an entire week celebrating our wedding with our family, and spent about half as much as a five hour wedding in Westchester would have cost. It was such an amazing experience - we could focus on each other, and the beginning of our life together, instead of on seating arrangements and bridesmaid dresses.

Now, we did have to compromise a bit. I come from a very big family and it was upsetting to me not to have all my cousins, aunts, uncles, grandparents, and friends there. And I know there were some hurt feelings. But ultimately it was about me and my husband, and we felt this was what we wanted the most. Neither of us regret a single moment of our wedding week (except for when we realized that my husband forgot his birth certificate and we almost couldn't get married, but that's a story for another day).

And the best part is when we returned from our honeymoon, we had a party with our family and closest friends to celebrate. I mean seriously, how many women get to wear their wedding dress twice? Who could ask for more!"
~Stacey

And yet another bride, who was totally satisfied with her destination wedding:

"I am blessed to report that my wedding went extremely well, both in the planning process as well as the actual day. I like to think that a great deal of weight was lifted off me because I chose to have a destination wedding. We had a relaxed and playful wedding that just felt like us, which is important when picking a venue. (I think that would be my #1 tip.) It is also the secret loop-hole regarding all guests you deem intolerable but feel you have to invite. The true loves of your life will make it there, especially if you give ample time for people to plan. But the ones you'd rather not invite have to understand that a destination wedding is usually pretty exclusive. Close friends and family in paradise, and if they argue otherwise, it's just tacky.

My wedding was budget-friendly, but that term is certainly relative. I believe that if you let yourself get caught up in wishing you had that or this, it can detract from your day as well as get you sidetracked. We did the best we could with what money we had and haven't really looked back. My advice *would be to take the time to think of creative ways to set your wedding apart, making it unique. I never look at a wedding after having mine and wish I had a bride's crystal or thousand dollar stilettos. What I sometimes wish I had thought about is playful poses or an artistic way of highlighting an easy DIY project gone perfect. Weddings are getting more and more un-traditional and I personally love it.*

My husband and I had a great adventure with the wedding process. My parents are divorced and it took 27 years and a wedding for them to act like adults. They showed their best faces for us. My mother-in-law helped with the photographer and rehearsal dinner. My father paid for the bulk of the wedding. My mother paid for the dress and the invites. We were so touched by how much support we had from everyone that it could not have been anything but a beautiful event." ~Claire

No matter what type of wedding you choose, my tip for you is to plan with your fiancé to stay together at your reception. This is crucial. Hold hands, have a buddy-system, a special secret code or wink or nipple squeeze. Whatever works. Just have some form of communication in place so that you both know when one of you needs to move on so you can bail each other out. Sure, you love everyone and are grateful they are celebrating with you, but if you let them keep talking or pull you in different directions, you'll get separated from your hubs. It will only be a matter of time before you find yourself in a corner choking on the smell of Uncle Barry's bad breath and Aunt Judy's eau de cigarette masking musk while catching far-off glances of your husband on the dance floor busting it out to your favorite song, wondering where the hell you went.

Seating Chart

When it's time to organize your seating chart, I recommend you do the following: Run yourself a nice, warm, bath. Play some mellow music, sniff some lavender oil, and do whatever you need to do to relax. Allow yourself no distractions. Once you are out of the bath and dry, it's time to tackle the chart. Here we go!

Step 1: Tie your hair back in a ponytail or a nice, tight bun, as this will help you refrain from ripping it the fuck out of your head.

Step 2: Grab one bottle of wine to get you through your side of the family's tables, and another bottle to get you through his. (Your friends are easy – just put them near the bar and/or dance floor.) Crack open that first bottle and pour yourself a glass.

Step 3: Call your mother, and your in-laws, and have them explain again why Aunt Josie and Uncle Frank's family can't be seated within three tables of each other, and why cousin Jeremy needs to be kept at a safe distance from both the dance floor and the waitstaff.

Step 4: Crack open the second bottle of wine too early. To hell with it.

Step 5: Look over your list of those lovely and considerate individuals who have yet to RSVP. Construct a voodoo doll in their form. Insert a few pins to relieve your stress. Seek comfort in the fact that this quite possibly could be working.

Lather, rinse, repeat.

Now that you have locked-in your date and have the major details of your hall in place, it's time to explore the other elements of your big day…

Table #8: The Dress

Trying on bridal gowns was a mixed experience for me. The first one or two were fun, but the process of getting in and out of these gargantuan and elaborate gowns became old quickly.

And getting into them was no party. Some of them you can maneuver stepping into, some you have to shimmy on, and some of them come with a pole vault and a can of WD-40. But my favorite had to be the ones that they throw over your head and pull over your body, hoping you are still breathing by the time you emerge. There you are, buck naked on a pedestal, a saleswoman coming at you with forty pounds of tooling. Before you know it, you are blinded by a tunnel of white and you can't see a damn thing. Between the birthday suit, the temporary blindness, and the faint and muffled sound of distant voices, I kept imagining this is what it might have felt like coming through the birth canal. Except here, there was a saleswoman at the end of the tunnel instead of a doctor.

Saleswoman: "Sweetie, can you see my hand?!"

Me: "Uh…No…" (slight panic)

Saleswoman: "I see your head…Grab on! Here we go! And…it's…ON! (*gush*) Oh, breathtaking! This is the one." Just like every other one I tried on.

The process can quickly lose its allure when you start looking at the price tags on the dresses, as well as the accessories that go along with them. Next time you are in a salon, watch what happens when a bride-to-be shows an inkling of interest in a dress she has tried on. Within a matter of seconds, the salespeople will fetch for her a veil, a tiara, a pair of shoes and a bridal party from the back room and adorn her with it all – you know, just so she can "get a feel for what it would look like." Of course, they are taking a chance at you purchasing other accessories to go along with your dress while they have you in that moment.

That's fine. This is sales, after all. But know that, as with most other forms of sales, your emotions are being capitalized on. Be prepared for them to tell you that you have to order your dress one year out and that you're running out of time. Brace yourself for the speech on the rarity of the gown, the high demand of the designer, and the "one-time-only dis-count" if you order it now and pay in full. Smile and nod, then don't be afraid to walk away, get some rest, do some research, and come back with a clear head. As is the case in many sales environments, commissions are abundant. I have met honest people who work in these salons that really take their jobs seriously. They see each bride as an individual and want to match her with a gown that fits her style and will look amazing on her. But these people are hard to come by, so buyer, beware.

Of course, shopping for your gown can and should be a great experience when shared with your mother, sister or anyone else close to you, because it is a big decision and a fun one at that. When I finally settled on a dress, it felt great to try it on for those near and dear to me. But while your search is on, don't ask for *too* many opinions. Regardless of your personal style, budget, or wedding date, take only those closest to you. Take Lisa's advice:

"Only go dress shopping with a select person or people. Do NOT make it a circus. I only went with my mom, sister & grandma. I would have brought my mother in law along but who needs somebody telling you why every dress doesn't look right (unless it's your sister, who has full license to say those things, and whom you trust will be honest?).

When I went with my sister to Kleinfeld's to pick out her dress, it was a great experience. She ordered a gorgeous Panina Tourneu gown, strapless, in a rich ivory color, with just the right amount of cascading flowers on the skirt. As would only happen at Kleinfeld's, Panina Tourneu herself was there that day, and saw my sister in the gown and offered her advice on alterations. It was unreal, and my sister "said yes." She was STUNNING! Everyone was happy.

On the day of the wedding, before the reception even began, one of those gorgeous little fabric flowers popped right off of her dress. You could imagine our dismay since not only did my sister pay a lot of money for that gown, but that something so important and well-made could have a mishap.

So don't always assume that the more you spend, the better the quality, because as you can see, nothing is perfect. And that is simply life – it happens. Flowers pop off. It pours on your wedding day. You can't take it too seriously.

But perhaps the worst part about the experience is that, after the wedding, my sister called Kleinfeld's to let them know about the flower debacle. She spoke to the saleswoman who assured her she would contact the manager and owner so they could "do the right thing" and help her out, possibly in the form of a complimentary preservation of the gown and a cleaning, or something along those lines – *and then they never called her back.* It stinks, but as many post-brides experience with their vendors, once they have your money, you are no longer priority.

Make sure when you put your gown on, you can still see yourself.

Back at Kleinfeld's, I saw something almost as wonderful as my sister when she found her gown. Amidst all of the blonde hair, the taffeta and the rhinestones, the "oohs" and "ahhs" coming from every bride-to-be's respective cronies, emerged something rather extraordinary.

Bopping out of the dressing room and bouncing through the center of the floor was a girl. She was no model. She was short and petite, with obviously dyed bright red hair cut into a bob. She had blue nails and red shoes, and was wearing a short white tutu style gown. She had tattoos on her forearms, and donned a small hat with old-fashioned netting.

Instantly, without trying, she commanded the attention of everyone on that floor and all of the mouths of the brides-to-be standing on their respective pedestals dropped open. She was gorgeous. It wasn't because she simply looked "different," and I certainly do not suggest that you should dye your hair bright red and go get tattoos before your wedding (and believe me, I don't want your mother or grandmother coming after me). The point is that the reason why this girl was so gorgeous, and every crazy thing she had on worked together for her in a beautiful harmony, is because you could tell that right down to her core, this girl was being *herself*.

Advice from a bridal shop employee

There I was at another bridal salon, this time as a bridesmaid for my best friend Judith. Judith got married on Cinco de Mayo, and if you knew Judith, you'd understand just how fitting a Cinco de Mayo wedding was for her. She is her own little version of Sofia Vergara: Mexican, gorgeous, and one of the funniest people I know. She wanted a dress that fit her personality, so we checked into Anjolique Bridal in Charlotte, N.C., and the search began.

I was prepared for the usual salespeople and their "been there, done that and know better" condescending approach, but as she started trying on dresses, something rather peculiar happened: The saleswoman actually was warm, and helpful. Sure, she wanted to make a sale, but she really took the time to offer great advice and get to the bottom of the type of dress my friend wanted. She asked great questions and was patient, and wasn't overboard with the "salesy" attitude.

One of the most helpful things she mentioned was that most brides ultimately wind up deciding between two dresses – usually two completely different styles. Judith found herself in exactly that situation. One dress was sexy and playful – it totally fit her style. But the traditional ball gown that I would have never pinned her for kept beckoning to her from the hanger. She kept trying the two on, and the saleswoman began to help even more, and you could tell she was sincere and genuine. Some of the questions she asked were:

- How do you feel in the dress?
- What side of yourself do you want to put forth on your wedding day?
- How do you want to present yourself to your husband?

These questions may seem obvious and simple, but ironically, this was the first time I had ever heard anyone ask them. Usually you hear:

- What is your budget?
- Where is your wedding going to be held?
- Do you want strapless or not?

Of course, these questions can be important as well. But they seem to stay on the surface, while the first set of questions manages to get down to another layer of ourselves. And chances are that answering these questions will determine the answers to the other ones, anyway. Because let's admit it:

Half the time, we don't even know what the hell it is that we want. Judith never thought she'd go for a ball gown, but when she tried one on for the heck of it, she saw herself in a different light – and loved it. So give several different styles a try.

I pictured myself in a trumpet-style gown with one shoulder, zero tooling under the skirt, and absolutely no beads (I hated beadwork). In the end, I found nothing I liked without beading, one shoulder wasn't cutting it, and the trumpet style on my five-foot-nothing frame made me look like a child making communion. Needless to say, I threw even myself for a loop when I wound up in a strapless gown, with tooling beneath the skirt, and beads covering every inch.

No matter what dress you decide to go with, stay true to your style. Think outside the box, and don't be afraid to take an unconventional approach. If a traditional white ball gown is what you feel wonderful in, stay true to that. But if it doesn't, don't feel you must follow a specific "bridal mold." Listen to that voice inside over all of the other influences and chatter going on. It's your wedding. Don't be afraid to make your own rules.

Put on a Pedestal

I'd like to take this moment to put my husband's sister on a pedestal. Although that's probably the last place she'd step.

She is one of the few women I know who got married and didn't have a herd of people following her while visiting the pricey bridal gown boutiques, being squeezed into every piece of glitter and tooling until she found "The One." No, not her. She grabbed her parents and went instead to an upscale department store. They sat there, skeptical, as she sifted through the standard "evening gowns" section. And when she pulled an unassuming white halter top dress from the racks, with a price tag reading much less than the cost of a gown sold by the traditional bridal boutiques, and headed for the dressing room, they didn't bat an eye. They suspected that her quest would be unfulfilled, and it was just a matter of time before they'd be heading off to Kleinfeld's.

And then. She emerged from the dressing room, positively glowing, and somehow this simple little dress was IT. Her parents instantly knew it as well, and just like that, the search was over. On the day of her wedding, I helped her fasten a beautiful silver broach from her grandmother to the center of the neckline. I was honored that she asked me to do her hair for her. I did so in a loose bun, with a few sprays of hairspray and some bobby pins. We plucked an orchid from her bouquet, and tucked it behind her ear.

She was stunning. Part of this was because it was her wedding day. But most of it was because she was *her natural self.*

Pretty Pretty Princesses: The Fairest of them All

"As with all of us, what I want for my daughter seems so simple: for her to grow up healthy, happy, and confident, with a clear sense of her own potential and the opportunity to fulfill it. Yet she lives in a world that tells her, whether she is three or thirty-three, that the surest way to get there is to look, well, like Cinderella." ~Peggy Orenstein, Author

While perusing through the library researching for this project, and after striking out for research in the "wedding" section, I wandered into the "women's" section. It was here that I stumbled upon a book called *Cinderella Ate My Daughter*, written by *New York Times* columnist Peggy Orenstein. It's a really interesting book, and if you have a little girl or are planning on doing so someday, it's definitely worth a read. But looking at it from the angle where I was standing, I almost couldn't believe it wasn't in the "wedding" section.

Orenstein, after having a daughter of her own, goes on a quest to see what effects the "princess" culture has on girls at a young age, as well as throughout their lives. The inside flap of the book explains:

"From premature sexualization to the risk of depression to rising rates of narcissism, the potential negative impact of this new girlie-girl culture is undeniable…"

It's tempting to think that girls outgrow the "princess" phase once they transition into adulthood, enter the job force and start paying bills. But does it really go away? Once wedding season kicks in, those tendencies tend to come rushing right back, and we see that the princesses in fact do still exist. They're just harder to spot, since they no longer walk around in sparkly hot pants carrying a pink lunch box in one hand and a fairy wand in the other (well, most of them, at least).

Consider how we are groomed from a young age to uphold a certain set of values and goals. Orenstein talks about the insane amount of ways that society begins to prep little girls to become princesses.

The classic example of the giant force that propels this idea is, of course, none other than the Disney franchise. So, Orenstein sat down with Disney executive Andy Mooney to discuss the birth of the princess craze. He explains how he went to a "Disney on Ice" show many years ago and saw several little girls walking around in home-made princess costumes. It suddenly dawned on him the incredible potential to market and sell a Princess line through Disney. He took his idea to the company and pitched it to the executives. As he explained to Orenstein:

> "It was a risky move: Disney had never marketed its characters sep-
> arately from a film's release, and old-timers like Roy Disney con-
> sidered it heresy to lump together those from different stories. That
> is why, these days, when the ladies appear on the same item, they
> never make eye contact. Each stares off in a slightly different direc-
> tion, as if unaware of the other's presence."

Orenstein comments in her book: "Now that I have told you, you'll always notice it. And let me tell you, it's freaky." Hmm. Not long after reading this, my husband and I were walking through the grocery store and saw a child's cup with the Disney Princesses on it. I looked closely and, just as Mooney explained, each of the princesses was pictured gazing off into a different direction, as if she stood alone.

Now, keeping that in mind, head over to Kleinfeld's one afternoon and observe the grown women, dressed in their ball gowns, standing on their respective pedestals. Notice how many of them are making eye contact with other brides-to-be, acknowledging and talking to each other. Yup. Fa-reaky.

I can't help but draw more parallels between little girls playing princess and adult women getting married. In terms of creating products and marketing toward young girls, Mooney tells Orenstein, "The counsel we gave to licensees was this: What type of bedding would a princess want to sleep in? What kind of alarm clock would a princess want to wake up to? What type of television would a princess like to see?" I wonder how much they sold this marketing plan to the places we register for wedding gifts.

Orenstein goes on to explain:

> "I do not question that little girls like to play princess: as a child, I certainly availed myself of my mom's cast-off rhinestone tiara from time to time. But when you're talking 26,000 items (and that's just Disney), it's a little hard to say where 'want' ends and 'coercion' begins. Mooney was prepared for that concern and for my overall discomfort with the Princesses, who, particularly in his consumer product versions, are all about clothes, jewelry, makeup, and snaring a handsome husband."

I don't think that all brides and everything wedding is about the "princess push" or propelled by the fact that we watched *Cinderella* as a kid. But I do think it's a huge trend that permeates every area of the wedding industry, and that the wedding marketers are eerily similar to the Disney marketers in terms of their message.

And we should probably try to stop it, at least for the adult women. As a bride, yes, it's your day. Sure, you are the rock star for twenty-four hours. It's a celebration! But if we are not careful, it can also take on a life of its own, and we can lose sight of what's really important and what makes us all unique.

I'm also not suggesting that you forego the entire wedding, or completely alter your plans or your thinking. (I certainly did not.) I'm simply suggesting that you make these connections and acknowledge them as you go through your planning process. Partly because I want you to make sure you are letting your own individuality shine through and not succumbing to a "mold" of what you think you should be, and partly because I want to prevent you from going off the deep end. We are all human, and we all are influenced by outside sources.

Dig deep down to find out what it is that you want for yourself, what it is that you and your spouse want, how you both want this day to go down. Think about what makes you, well, YOU, and what makes your relationship unique. Remember that you don't have to do things a certain way because that's what marketers tell you, it's what you think you should do, or it's what you see everyone around you doing. Push all that other crap and expectations to the side, ask yourself questions to get down to the root of what is truly important to you, and remember that there are no rules.

You are going to be gorgeous on your wedding day, there is no question about that. But staying true to yourself will ensure you'll radiate all that gorgeousness from the inside-out.

Back to the Dais: All you need is love?

Does love keep a marriage together? Or does marriage keep love together? This is a question that therapist Leslie Petruk, a Licensed Professional Counselor who has worked with many couples, overheard an individual ask a pastor during a sermon.

It seems simple enough, but it's a very profound question when you break it down and think about it.

The logic is normally that, of course, love keeps a marriage together. But dig a bit deeper, and you realize that the "feeling" of love does not exist every single day of your wedded life. Instead, the pastor answered that it is in fact the covenant of *marriage* that keeps the *love* going. You make a promise to each other, you work on yourselves and your relationship and, as a result, you continue to nurture your love. It's a frame of mind. You have to water that seed and weed that garden. Making a commitment to each other helps you work to strengthen that bond you share.

There are mornings you are going to wake up, and you aren't going to be brimming with love. There are mornings you will wake up, and you might not even feel you *like* the person next to you. And that's okay. If you find yourself bored and convincing yourself that you "love the person, but are not in love with the person anymore," consider the fact that this may be because the honeymoon period has ended. "What do you mean? Marriage isn't all shits and giggles?!" Nope. And if you quit one to jump into another, you may find that once the honeymoon phase wears off in your new marriage, you are going to go through the same thing with someone else.

Leslie weighs in about the delusion of the "forever honeymoon" phase: "That's not real life. That might be movie land…You have to work at marriage, and it's not a feeling. It's an action. Love is an action. You're not going to walk in the door and feel this immense passion for your partner every day."

So what can you do if you are stuck in a rut? The answer may not be to enroll in couple's therapy. Instead, you have to do one of the most difficult things we could possibly do, and that is to look internally, identify the issues you have lurking around in yourself, and work on those first. You owe it to both yourself and your partner to give this a try. As Leslie explains, "It's a process…When individuals do their own therapy, a lot of times their marriage just gets better without even doing couples counseling. Looking at their own wounds helps them understand each other on a whole other level…The irony is that once they are done working on themselves, they often build such a better understanding of one another that they don't even need couples therapy."

"Success in marriage does not come merely through finding the right mate, but through being the right mate." ~Barnett R. Brickner

Love is a Drug

We've heard people say before, and may have said ourselves, that love is a drug - and that really is no bullshit. The act of falling in love literally creates symptoms in our brains that are similar to those that certain drugs can create. Drs. Tom and Bev Rogers explore this topic, dubbed the "Love Cocktail," further:

> "Research shows that when a person falls in love, or trips into infatuation, his or her brain is flooded with chemicals. These include norepinephrine, epinephrine, dopamine, and especially phenylethylamine, PEA for short. These chemicals make up what Michael Liebowitz from the New York Psychiatric Institute calls, 'the love cocktail.' Symptoms from these neurotransmitters working in concert are: a delightful positive attitude, increased energy and decreased need for sleep, loss of appetite, and general euphoria. Wow, who wouldn't want a hit of that?!...This explains why we have such an altered physical state when we fall in love. It also helps us to put the notion of falling in love into a more clear and rational perspective."

We can, and totally should, enjoy the high, but understanding what it is will help us realize that when it wears off, it doesn't mean we "don't love someone" anymore. If you become addicted to the "love cocktail," just like a drug addict, you will spend much of your life chasing that next high, grasping for a constant state of euphoria and its unattainable permanence.

Addicts of any kind have two choices: either get clean, or wait for the inevitable overdose and demise. The same holds true for "love" addicts: work on your relationship after the drug wears off, or keep chasing "hits," overdose, and suffer the consequences. The choice is yours.

That's not to say that you should stay in an abusive relationship or with a partner who does not value you as a person. Just be careful that you aren't contemplating leaving a relationship because that "honeymoon" feeling is no longer there, and falling for the old "grass is greener" fallacy. Bev explains, "Studies show that every couple has three major issues they fight about. If you trade partners, you just trade issues."

Leslie weighs in again: "We all come with our baggage, and there is going to come a point, usually in mid-life, that all of that is going to come to the surface. You're going to try to blame it on your spouse, if you aren't ready to deal with it yourself, and you may go your own way – and it's going to happen all over again. Or, you're going to deal with yourself, and work through it, and work through the partnership issues, and deepen and strengthen the intimacy and connection in your own marriage." She explains that many times in therapy, couples point fingers at what is wrong with their spouse. That's fine, but she has found that when couples branch off to work on themselves first, they understand each other more.

Yes, the wonderful, glorious feeling of love that you have in the beginning – the "Love Cocktail" – is going to subside. But wait! Back yourself away from that ledge and drop that noose for this little nugget of wisdom from Tom and Bev: When we nurture a relationship over the long term and *commit* ourselves to another, there is indeed a reward.

"Oxytocin is a chemical that is released many times when long-term couples make love. Many scientists call it the 'cuddle chemical.' It gives couples a sensation that all is right with the world. So, you see, if you hang on after the phenylethylamine has faded, you will get the chance to take advantage of one of nature's other more soothing remedies. Commitment does have its rewards."

See? Just when you thought you were all "peace, love and Jesus" for getting hitched, you find out you really are all "sex, drugs and rock n' roll" – and you don't even need to leave home to get it.

Table #9: Vendors

The financial aspect of a wedding is like a chess game with not enough pieces. And instead of harmless horses and knights to dodge, you'll find emotion-sucking villains. They come in the form of bridesmaidzillas, in-laws, crazy guests and salespeople. But atop your chessboard of chaos, you may also encounter some pretty unreliable and overpriced vendors.

Be ever so careful when choosing vendors and making decisions for your wedding. Plenty of vendors love what they do and have great business ethics, but sadly, for every one of those there are three who will screw you over and leave you high and dry at a moment's notice. It's hard to find the diamond in the rough. Lisa weighs in:

"Do your homework, and trust your gut. Vendors will always glorify themselves and make you feel like they are better than everybody else in the industry. If you feel that smoke is being blown up your ass, or it's all too good to be true, it probably is! Ask for samples, and definitely shop around. They will always make you feel that time is limited, so you will book faster. Trust me, when a vendor's work speaks for itself, they don't need to do this. Talk to someone that you know is savvy and can help you."

Choosing your vendors wisely can be a difficult task. They often come with hefty price tags, and you are left to weigh how you can stretch your budget to accommodate your wants. You are paying them for a service, and a luxury service at that. We all know that these types of services can be pricey.

While vendors are pros at dealing with brides, brides have little-to-no experience dealing with vendors. Quite the contrary: A bride is making many different decisions in areas that are foreign to her, all at the same time, for one day in her life. Finances are tight, the clock is ticking, and the pressure is on. All of these factors create a set of circumstances that make it extremely easy for a bride to be taken advantage of, and unfortunately, some vendors capitalize on this. So it's important to do some research in your area to find reputable vendors who are worth the expense. If you are not careful, you could be taken for a ride. Take Tonya's nightmare with her videographer, for example:

"I booked him a year in advance because he was supposedly 'the best in town'. Two months before my wedding I decided to contact him to make sure everything was set. I remembered him saying when we booked that he wanted to meet my husband 3 months before and ask us some questions in person so that he would add them into the video. When I tried to get in touch with him, he didn't return any of my phone calls. This went on for about a month. His voice mail was full over and over again. So finally, with one month to go before my wedding and after already paying a deposit, I started calling other videographers in town to see if they knew him or where he was. No one knew. Finally, my photographer actually gave me a contact of someone who knew him personally. They said he was joining up with another videographer in town. So finally after still not being called back I had my mother-in-law call the owner of the new company. Can we say, stalkers? Yep, that's what we were. But I truly feel that if we didn't stalk him, that a videographer would not have shown up on our wedding day. Anyway, to say the least he has been a nightmare to work with ever since. He did show up on that day thank goodness. But he has no communication skills whatsoever. He told us we would get our video three months after our wedding and we're going on four now and guess what? No video! He just keeps telling me to be patient and that it will be worth the wait. Let's hope so!"

Now, all vendors aren't nightmares, of course. I know and have personally experienced many vendors who are not only exceptional at what they do, but who love their jobs as well. My goal here is to help you find similar vendors near you, help you make better decisions, ask the right questions, and not pay for service that isn't up to par.

Also, prepare yourself for the shock at what vendors may cost. Once you see the endless possibilities along with their accompanying price tags, you can't help but wonder, "But so-and-so had this at their wedding! How were they able to do that?" Because they are probably in fucking debt up to their eyeballs, that's how! Try to resist the urge to compete, and don't do anything that will cause you added stress long after your wedding.

Do what works for you, spend your money where you feel it is most important, and stick to what you truly can manage. Some of the most beautiful weddings have been planned on a strict budget, and the resources available for great ideas and inexpensive personal touches are endless.

Photographer and Videographer

When my husband and I got married, we made a list of the most important things to spend our money on: photographer, videographer, food, and entertainment. We both felt that if you hire a great photographer and videographer, they will capture your memories for you to cherish. And if you provide great food and entertainment, your guests will truly enjoy your wedding.

On a random stroke of fate, we found a photographer who was the son of the man who photographed my parents on their wedding day thirty-seven years earlier. For us, it was pretty much a done deal before we had even seen his work, as you could imagine how caught up we were in the novelty of the situation. He would take traditional photos, make a beautiful album, and everything would be fabulous. He did, he did, and it was. But he also was charging three months' salary and our firstborn child. When all was said and done, we were left wondering if spending that money was really worth it.

For starters, it was pouring rain on our wedding day, so heavy that we could not even take pictures outside. Alas, the gorgeous, vibrantly-colored fall photos that I envisioned for my October wedding would not come to be; instead, my football team of a bridal party would huddle at the church altar for an array of photo sessions my photographer desperately tried to make interesting. Sure, he got some nice pictures. But even if the weather was gorgeous that day, would it have been worth it? Certainly you want pictures. But should we have considered another option, rather than spend so much money?

In my family, it's a tradition to throw the bride and groom an engagement party, and we were no exception. Around the same time of our party, my brother had met a photographer who was taking pictures of his band. At the last minute we asked the photographer if he would be willing to come to our engagement party and take some pictures, and he agreed. We bought him dinner and paid him $150 – and his pictures were awesome. AWESOME. No fancy website, no contract, no problem. He did not provide us with an album, but guess what? We had a computer and an internet connection. We got online and created our own album. You can do this too if your budget is tight, and I bet you probably have a buddy who is a pro in design willing to help you lay it out. Many design programs are so easy that the process is as simple as "drag and drop." Add quotes, favorite sayings, or even phrases from cards that guests gave to you. Better yet, add your honeymoon photos and have an all-in-one kick-ass wedding album.

The great part about this approach is that not only would it be totally custom and personal, but you'll also get to include pictures taken by guests at your wedding. I remember when booking our wedding photographer, I didn't pay much attention to the fact that the moment our cake was cut, he would pack it up and head out. This is the case with most vendors, and it makes sense on their part. At the very end of the night, the band continued to play, and all the remaining guests had another dance party before leaving. It was great, and I remember that part of the night more than any other. But since our photographer and video crew had already bounced, I had no professional footage. Luckily, one of my friends took a few candid shots and videos with her camera. I love her shots just as much, if not more, than the formal shots.

Gone are the days of the traditional coffee table album with the tired metallic binding as a staple. If super-fancy is your style, go for it, but explore the options and think outside the box just a bit to let your personal style shine through. I promise you will love the results, and your wallet will thank you.

If you are going to hire both a videographer and photographer, find out whether they've worked together in the past. If you hire a photographer first, ask him if there is a particular videographer he works well with, and vice versa. Chances are, he or she can recommend someone. The last thing you want is two people you have never met before fighting on the dance floor to get the best shots, or becoming frustrated with the work style of the other. This happens. Egos may fly. And you and your groom will sadly be the ones affected.

Learn from Denise (and her bi-polar photographer)

"I went to a specific local photographer because I heard they could wonderfully photograph the City Club, in Charlotte, NC, where we were to be married. What I didn't know was that it was the husband, not his wife that had the experience with the City Club. The day we went there we met and hired the wife, not knowing she had never shot a wedding there before.

"As I have been for most every event of mine I was a little late to my own wedding! The photographer was there one hour before me as per my instructions to shoot everyone else getting ready. We were to be married at 7 pm, just as the sun was setting over the city. I arrived with my bridesmaids, mom and mom-in-law with only 20 minutes until the sunset. Just enough time to get a few shots of me alone and a few of me with my bridesmaids (only three of them).

She was a BITCH from the second I walked in. I said 'HI!' all happy and excited to see her. She looked at me kind of blank and started talking really fast and nervous. I was not nervous, just happy and excited. I told her it was fine, I only need two or three shots of me which took her all of three minutes. My girls were trying to tell me to stand up straight because I was hunched over and she yelled at them- 'You girls are OUT OF CONTROL!' We all stood there looking at each other in shock. Did my photographer just yell at me and my bridesmaids on my wedding day?! Determined to stay in my happy place I ignored her, we finished the shots and we walked down the aisle on time. The sun was setting glorious oranges, yellows and purples across our faces as we said 'I do.' It was perfect. After the ceremony, I asked (yes, I had to ask) the photographer to take a few pics of me and my husband. She seemed annoyed! We went over to the window and she took exactly two pictures and then walked off. Well, I thought to myself, the night is just beginning; there will be plenty of time for pictures! As we made our way to the cocktail hour in the large room adjacent us, my mom and father-in-law both informed us that they had asked the photographer to take pictures of them before I had arrived to which she snapped 'Denise does not want posed pictures!' I had asked her to do more photojournalist type pics and minimal posed ones with the understanding that some of them HAVE to be posed. I was shocked again by her behavior.

"After the cocktail hour we were introduced by the band, ate our dinner and proceeded to dance. I just kept thinking to myself, 'Where is the photographer? Why hasn't she taken many pictures of us?' I spotted her standing on the edge of the dance floor NOT taking pictures so I bounded cheerfully up to her (and anyone who knows me knows this is my normal way of being-I do not lie!) I said-and I QUOTE 'Would you mind taking some pictures of Brian and I now? All the formalities are over and we can slip away for a few minutes.' She yelled in my face 'I GOT IT!' Again...shock. I stumbled away from her not sure what to say.

"I decided to not let it ruin our day. I was having a blast listening to my now husband sing 'Brown Eyed Girl' to me with the band and it again occurred to me that the night was almost over and we really needed to get some pictures together. I went up to her again, smiling this time but too scared to be my bubbly self. I said, 'We are going to be leaving soon, could you please take a *few quick shots of us together?' She yelled in my face again 'I GOT IT!' I should have insisted, asked her what her problem was or just bitch slapped her (OK maybe not that last one) but I just shut down, unable to even process what had just happened.*

*"When we returned from our glorious two week Mediterranean cruise and went in to see the pictures, I cried. There were (as I had suspected) only a few of the two of us and some of them were out of focus. **They kept trying to talk us into having a 'do over' at the City Club! How can you recreate your wedding day?** You CANNOT! In the end they refunded us $500.00 and they had to use many of the candid pictures our friends had taken that night to even make an album. What is the moral of the story? Well, if there is one I think it would be...don't be afraid to stand up for yourself, and to demand your vendors do what they were paid for. I should have been more aggressive-or at least told someone and let THEM be aggressive!*

"Luckily, we had one friend who took phenomenal candid shots, so when I look back on our pictures I can only smile and remember how beautiful and full of love the day was. Perfect in every way." -Denise

Moral of the story: No matter whose fault it was, you don't get a do-over. Go the extra mile with your homework because some vendors are just downright egotistic and sheisty. Oh, and make sure your photographer takes her meds in the morning.

As we all know, your pictures will last a lifetime, and because of this it's easy to hold high expectations and put pressure on ourselves to get everything right. But pressure creates stress, and neither of these result in relaxation or calm. Tension or anxiety will show up in pictures, because the camera doesn't lie. Because of this, find a photographer with whom you are comfortable. This is just as important as the backdrop they will use and their creative portfolio. The photographer's ability to put you at ease and let your guard down is truly what will give you amazing pictures.

If your wedding comes and goes and you find you are less than satis-fied with your pictures, don't beat yourself up. Remember that some of the best pictures of you and your spouse are still to come. Some of my favorite pictures are of the everyday moments that my husband and I have shared, that don't involve an expensive dress or a choreographed series of poses. I treasure these just as much as my wedding photos.

For me, one in particular comes to mind. We were in an apple orchard in Newport, Rhode Island. While walking along we ducked under a tree, my husband held out the camera and we smiled. My hair is up (which I hate), we aren't posing, but it's perfect. You'll have plenty of these opportunities, and your wedding is just the beginning. Happiness is spontaneous and free.

Wedding Cake

You may have visions of a nineteen-tier wedding cake with sugar-plums and butter cream dancing all around it, and that's all good. But really research your available bakeries, and don't just order on a whim. Take Kelly's experience:

"Our experience with our cake vendor seemed to be a great one at first. We were so impressed with him, his photos of previous cakes and his overall professionalism. Not to mention the samples we tasted were amazing! We decided on an elegant four-tiered buttercream frosted cake with alternating chocolate crème and raspberry filled center.

"All we talked about for months was this cake and how we couldn't wait to see it in all its glory and taste its ever-so-sweet simplicity. The time came to make our grand entrance to the reception, and my mom rushed over and pulled me aside. She wanted to give me a heads-up that our cake was not four-tiered, but rather six! My first thought – "Two tiers for free, now that's what I'm talking about." Finally, something that didn't cost extra! Without notice, I was quickly whisked away from her before she could tell me the rest of the story.

"We were happily introduced as man and wife and without delay, noticed what was right in front of us – the centerpiece of the room: our cake, leaning like the Tower of Pisa. This thing was gonna go at any minute and we still had to have our first dance, Father-Daughter dance and Mother-Son dance. There was no way. We nervously watched during our dance, not taking our eyes off of it. We were just waiting for it to slide right onto the floor in a pile of sugar and icing. Even the lead singer of the band noticed. He would look at the cake and look at us with the same thoughts we had. After only a minute into our dance, we gave him the go-ahead to cut the song short.

Now, I will be the first to say that I generally sprint anytime there's a cake in front of me, but I've never moved like I did towards that cake, weighed down by pounds of dress and all. We quickly snapped a few stereotypical cake photos while everyone watched nervously. Before the knife had been pulled from its first cut, the wedding director stepped in and disassembled it layer by layer with ninja speed, avoiding the "cakastrophe."

The lesson here, just like in life: You can have your cake and eat it too, but it just may end up on the floor."

It's also worth mentioning that once the cake leaves the bakery, they've done their job and it's out of their hands. Confirm with your reception hall that they have the accommodations to house the cake until you need it so that it doesn't melt or topple over during your celebration.

Flowers

Again, go back to your budget and see how important flowers are on your list. Do NOT walk into a florist blind and let them show you centerpieces because chances are you will fall in love with a crazy contraption that will make you throw up in your mouth when you hear the price.

Ask a trusted friend or family member who has been married recently, and is open and honest with you about prices, who they used for their florist. Schedule a meeting, but first get online and print out a few ideas to help the florist get a feel for what you want. You can save money by asking what is in season at the time of your wedding, since those flowers are usually less expensive.

Keep in mind when you are looking at centerpieces that you will also need your bouquet as well as your bridesmaids', boutonnieres for your hubby and the groomsmen, flower girl/ring bearer flowers, bouquets or corsages for the mothers of the bride and groom and, if applicable, flower arrangements for the church. Most florists offer you package deals, but keep these other expenses in mind so you don't blow your flower budget on the centerpieces.

My mom does floral designs for weddings, so I got lucky in this department. We had five different styles of centerpieces for the twenty-two tables in the room. There were trees on some of the tables. *Trees*, goddammit. The room was so gorgeous when we walked in. I cannot imagine what the price tag would have been had my mom not had the hookup.

While researching flowers for my wedding I compiled my own list of what different flowers symbolize.

Meaningful Flowers:

Almond blossom: hope
Apple blossom: good fortune
Calla Lilies: magnificent beauty
Camellia: gratitude
Carnation: fascination
Chrysanthemum (red): I love you
Chrysanthemum (white): truth
Cyclamen: modesty
Daffodil: regard

Daisy: innocence
Fern: fascination
Forget-me-not: remembrance
Gardenia: joy
Heather: good luck
Heliotrope: devotion
Honeysuckle: generosity
Hyacinth: loveliness
Ivy: fidelity
Iris: burning love
Japonica: loveliness
Jasmine: amiability
Lemon blossom: fidelity in love
Lilac: youthful innocence
Lily: majesty
Lily-of-the-valley: return of happiness
Magnolia: perseverance
Myrtle: love
Orange blossom: purity
Orchid: beauty
Peach blossom: captive
Rose: love, happiness
Snowdrop: hope
Sweat pea: pleasure
Tulip (red): I love you
Tulip (white): I am worthy of you
Tulip: love
Veronica: fidelity
Violet: faithfulness

Since the flowers were my mother's department, I let her take the lead and run with this one. But if I had to design my bouquet today based on this list, I would have:

Apple blossoms, daisies, and ferns, mixed with honeysuckle and magnolias, with cascading ivy.

Think Local

Look into options for local and independent vendors. Local vendors and small businesses can sometimes accommodate you far better than factories and larger companies. Maybe a nearby small business can create fabulous invitations for you. A local designer may be able to help you with a custom veil. You will find that the local places will be way more eager to help you, make your day personal, and do right by you, and at the same time, you are helping your community grow. Again, do some homework first to make sure the business has a clean record, and always go with your gut.

Once you have chosen your vendors, signed contracts, and fallen in love with how wonderful they will make your wedding, remember to feed them. I can't tell you how many times I've heard brides taken aback by this. "Oh, you have to…*feed* them, too?" No, they are actually a rare hybrid of a human that can last fourteen hours without requiring food while following you around all day! For cryin' out loud, give them a meal.

Ask your caterer what the deal is for vendors; usually, they charge half-price for each person instead of full. Every little bit counts. But the last thing you want to hear on your big day is a large *thud* as your video guy hits the ground, passed out from hunger, or to have some of your shots missed because the assistant had to make a Burger King run.

Invitations

Find an invitation that doesn't have a ton of inserts. It just looks better (and yes, it saves trees). Some people don't spend much time fussing over invitations; they just go to a store, pick a design and place the order. Others research and analyze every last detail because they perceive the invitation to be the first impression of their wedding, something that will set the tone for the entire event.

One of my friends was extremely meticulous about her invitations, agonizing over everything from font style, material, and color hues. Give it some thought, sure, and if you truly enjoy it, spend as much time as you like, but don't make yourself nuts. You've got plenty of other things to focus on. Another friend decided to have everyone RSVP online by directing them to a wedding website she created, since she felt that invitations are a waste because they go directly into the garbage. Everyone is different. Decide how you feel, pick an approach, and proceed.

I got my invitations from a vendor on Etsy.com where you'll find a ton of cool options, all handmade. However, I need to put in a big disclaimer here: Be careful if you take this route. I failed to do a background check. While they did a great job and designed a gorgeous invitation, I ran into a problem: While putting them in the mail, some of the envelopes started to come apart. Two turned into four, four turned into eight, and before we knew it, the ladies in the post office had the glue guns out to help us put them back together. I tried to contact the vendor, and their answer to me was that they order their envelopes from a separate paper supplier, and they would not take any responsibility. No refund, no apologies. Luckily, it all worked out, thanks to the ladies in the post office and my mom to the rescue, but I would never recommend using an unfamiliar company without doing a background check first.

Entertainment

You may already have an idea as to whether you'd like a band to play at your wedding or if you'd like a deejay, but do yourself a favor and keep an open mind before you book anything. We were sure we wanted a deejay and didn't give a band much thought. But then my dad (who is a musician) mentioned that he knew a guy who was part of a phenomenal wedding band and that we should check them out.

So Greg and I went one night to a showcase in the basement of one of the band member's homes, basically to humor my dad and get him off of our backs. We sat on the couch with our arms folded. "How long would this take?" we wondered. I reached in my bag to check my cell phone – and then the music started. We were both completely blown away. I had forgotten how much I enjoyed live entertainment like that, and before the first song was over, we had changed our minds. We booked them on the spot.

Whether you choose a band or a deejay, keep the following in mind:

*Will they play during your cocktail hour?
*How many hours is the contract for?
*Is there an emcee?
*Will they be interacting with the crowd?

In the end, we loved our wedding band. We paid a pretty penny for them, but for us it was worth it. Since entertainment was on our high-priority list, we budgeted accordingly. The band had four singers, various instruments and a horn section, and they mingled with the crowd on the dance floor. The fact that our guests crowd-surfed one of the singers was a testament to how much they enjoyed them, too.

Transportation

Whether you have visions of arriving in a traditional limo, on the back of a motorcycle, in a vintage car or by horse-drawn carriage, decide how you and your bridal party will get to the ceremony site. Get a party bus or limo that can hold a few more people than you will be having, so you are not on top of each other. You will want to allow yourself some space to kick back and relax, without having to worry about your drunken cousin spilling his vodka cranberry all over your gown.

If you and your guests will be staying at a nearby hotel after the reception, call that hotel and see if they provide a shuttle service to pick your guests up. Some will do this, others will not. I did not think about this, and found out later that my hotel did not provide a shuttle. At the last minute, we had to book a separate vendor, and it was a decent chunk of money we hadn't anticipated spending.

Favorite Websites

Here is a list of websites that I found helpful during my planning:

www.weddingbee.com – Really cute site that has a discussion board

www.liweddings.com – A Long-Island NY-based site with a TON of ideas

www.brides.com – A site which tends to have very original ideas

www.theknot.com – This one may be obvious to many, but it's a great resource

www.foreverandalways.com – Favor and gift ideas

www.etsy.com – I found my invitations here. It's not a bridal website; it sells all things handmade and is a great resource for gifts, invitations, or anything unique. They also have a wedding website: www.etsy.com/weddings.

http://www.myfairytaleaffairs.com - I got my scroll seating chart here. They also do invitations.

www.weddingwire.com – Good site for choosing music

www.originalrunners.com – Unique runners for the ceremony

www.retailmenot.com – Coupon site to find bargains

As a final note when it comes to your vendors, remember Gina's advice:

"Everyone will be nice to you until they have your money. They will answer all your questions and make time to meet with you. Then you pay them and suddenly they aren't as available and certainly not as accommodating. Always remember you are PAYING them, they are not doing you any favors here. Ask every single question you want to ask and don't let anyone make you feel bad about it. It's their job to help you. Don't let anyone intimidate you."

Well said! I certainly had my own eye-opening experiences with some vendors. Certain things fell by the wayside, and I felt the consequences.

Remember, this is your one and only big day, but to your vendors, this is also a business. And like any business, the focus is often on new customers and growing profits.

Do your best to choose the greatest vendors you can for your budget, and when you have booked them for your date and have everything in place, don't stress anymore. Pictures and video are priceless, and will live on for years to come, which is why we shell out a pretty penny for them (and rightfully so). The great vendors do exceptional work.

But never lose yourself in stress over trying to get everything perfect, or pressure yourself that this is your one shot to do so. You will never get to recreate your wedding day, but instead of letting this fact stress you out, use it to enjoy all of those beautiful pictures you take and just relax and have fun. The morning of your wedding, when you open your eyes, realize that this is it – you worked your ass off, and now it's here. Don't get lost in trying to control things to the point that you aren't living in the moment. What will be, will be, so allow the day to unfold and enjoy every waking minute of it.

Table # 10:
Bridal Showers and Big Box Marts

Registry and "Stuff"

It is the job of many in the retail industry to romanticize products and encourage you to make purchases, whether it's a new TV, the latest Botox injection, a new car, the new crash diet, and of course, the whale of them all - the fanciest wedding. Case in point: bridal gift registries.

It's a well-known fact that we often make purchases based on emotions rather than reason. Weddings take the cake in that department. We are human, and subconsciously or consciously, it happens. But during your planning, use caution when registering for gifts and entering the "big box marts," a.k.a. the giant department stores that we purchase our home items from.

"But what do you *mean*?" You say. "They invited me for a super-duper exclusive brunch! They are going to give me mimosas! And free books on what to register for that can double as nifty photo albums when I'm done! I need bedding! And plates! And I've been eyeballing those champagne flutes for a year!"

That's all good and fine, and you can certainly put those on your registry. But understand that people are employed, some making hundreds, thousands, even millions of dollars to steal your attention and get you to buy their products. This is okay because it is business, and we need business to make the world go round. But make it *your* business to know what you really need versus what will complicate your life, become wasteful, or stress you out. Looking at things from the other side will help you strike that balance and live somewhere between "Excitement-land" and "Realistic-ville." Registries should not be cookie-cutter. So, seriously - if you aren't into baking, put down the damn cookie cutters.

You probably don't need twelve crystal white wine goblets, twelve crystal red wine goblets, twelve casual white wine goblets, and twelve casual red. Even if you had that many people over simultaneously slugging vino, they'd probably be just fine using any type of cup. And ask yourself: Where the hell are you going to store all of these items when they aren't in use?

Drop the scanner, grab a beer

The day had come for Greg and I to register for our wedding gifts, and we headed into Fortunoff's in White Plains, N.Y. Upon our arrival, we were quickly whisked away into a side office. We were seated with an immaculately-dressed woman who gave us a crash course on all the items we "needed," along with a mini-binder packed with information on everything from china patterns to garbage cans.

After a conversation on what we should be looking for and a brief explanation of how the registry works, we were handed the sacred scanning device and sent on our merry way. The door closed behind us and there we stood, facing outward, amidst a sea of expensive china. (By the way, it's no mistake that this is where they start you off.) "Where do you want to start?" I asked my future hubs. After a long pause and a head scratch he said, "Hmm. I don't know. You?"

"Not sure." Long pause. Slight panic attack.

"There's a lot of stuff here."

"Yeah." Big exhale.

"Hey, you wanna go grab a beer?"

"Um, sure." We turned in our scanners to a dumbfounded employee and out we went, hand in hand.

I'm not really sure what happened there on that sales floor. I realize that many a woman in my shoes would have grabbed that scanner and ran like hell around that store, putting item after item on their wish list. I was watching them do it. I wanted to *want* to do it. But there was a nagging sense deep down inside of me, telling me that I didn't need half of the stuff that was on my nifty little list.

Would I really use all of these things, even if I didn't necessarily need them? I didn't think so. They would probably just take up space in my home and cause me stress while trying to figure out where to store it all. Where would all of it eventually wind up? The most obvious answer would be in my kitchen drawers, or in a closet, in storage, or maybe back to the store if I decided to make returns.

But I was also taking it to the next level. Eventually, all of these items that I truly didn't need would wind up in a landfill somewhere, because most items today truly are not made to withstand the test of time and are not built to be passed on to the next generation. Last but not least, what did any of this stuff have to do with marrying my best friend? Absolutely nothing.

I told my mom what happened, and that I was going to make a very small registry. She laughed at me. "What will people bring you?!" I come from a large Italian family, and there were close to one hundred ladies being invited to my shower. She had every right to laugh. And to be truthful, I had to laugh at myself for a second. I had gone from one extreme to another and that is usually never a good thing. I didn't want to be wasteful and register for a ton of crap. But I also realized that mama needed towels, silverware, and a decent blender.

"Fine," I said. "But I would really like it if you let people know on the invitations that I don't want them to wrap their gifts. It's a waste." My mom thought it would be rude to put that on the invitation. I fought, but I did not win. The ball was already rolling. And with all of the other decisions I was not prepared for, at this point, I was picking my battles.

With that, the big shower was planned, all of the invitations went out, and it quickly took on a life of its own. I loved my shower! But in terms of a take-away here, it's this: Think about the type of shower you'd like to have and what you'd truly like the experience to be. Those closest to you will probably have the best of intentions – I know my mom and sister did, and they truly threw me one hell of a shower. But they can't know exactly what you are thinking if you don't tell them. And by tell, I mean politely suggest, not dictate or demand. I had an absolutely wonderful shower and am grateful for every guest and every gift, and couldn't have asked for more. But if I had thought about it ahead of time and had spoken up, I could have maybe asked for *less*.

Greg and I eventually did wind up back in the stores, scanner in hand, picking out items to build the foundation of our lives together. But it was helpful to step out of the situation when we knew we would be overwhelmed. If you're wandering aimlessly and confused around Bed Bath and Beyond equipped with a scanning device, put the scanner down and step away slowly. If you are registering for that avocado pit extractor because you know that a) you will use it every day and b) it will undoubtedly shave precious minutes from your dinner or lunch routine, then go for it and don't let me stop you. Otherwise, cross it off your list - you don't need it. In fact, I am guessing that most women who have registered for this device have either returned it, or have it collecting dust in their kitchen drawer.

Our lives are very busy, so take a step back to evaluate what it is that you *really* need - what your *soul* really needs - and you'll find that it doesn't involve much of what we fill our lives with. We aren't equipped to deal with all of the information, tasks and expectations being thrown at us on a daily basis. No matter how "together" anyone else may seem, or how much we are expected or fake to be, we are really just a bunch of hot messes doing the best we can. As a matter of fact, much of what we fill our lives with is actually chipping away at our souls and our well-being.

So before you go scanning the entire kitchen department of your favorite store, zoom out for a moment. Picture how these items will fit into both your cabinets and your life, and assess what you both really could use. Resist the urge to succumb to the sweet seduction of marketing. Save the romanticism for the bedroom, not the sales floor.

Organize before you register to assess what you need

It's a good idea to get organized before you register for gifts so you can get a better idea of what you really need. When organizing and de-cluttering, I tend to use three piles: need it, love it, and launch it. Items that I truly need should by all means have a place in my home, and I find that place for those items. Some items that are decorative or sentimental get a free pass as well. But other than that, I try to not allow other items to clutter up my life.

It's a work in progress, but it's essential to ensure a stress-free, clutter-free environment – and mental state. We may not realize or make the connection as to how much time we spend looking for things or how frustration can negatively affect us when we open a messy kitchen drawer full of items we will never use, or try to find a pair of shoes in a disorganized closet, but after a while, the chaos starts to wear on us. A little simplicity goes a long way.

I am not suggesting that brides do not register. I certainly did, and am grateful for the gifts I received at my shower. If you are going to be living in your own home for the first time, it makes sense to register and it can be very practical. There are things you will need, and you are fortunate enough that you can have a shower in the first place. Just remember the above and keep yourself in check so you don't go overboard. Register for sanity; return the chaos.

And ask yourself, "Do I really need a shower?"

"If there is anything I hate it is WASTE! Which is pretty much the motivating factor of why I chose not to have a bridal shower. I had already been living in my own place for five years, which means I had spent five years cooking, bathing myself, and having gatherings at my place. What else could I possibly need to carry out these tasks? Nothing. Even better question, if I had a bridal shower and received all new stuff, what would I do with all my old stuff? It would become WASTE and I just couldn't deal with that." ~Leah

A tool that may help put things into perspective and decide how much you really need is this little video right here (link below). Take a minute to pull up your computer and have a look:

http://www.storyofstuff.com/

This little video influenced me and always makes me think twice about my purchases and what we are contributing to.

And even if you don't care about any of that, consider the fact that the more crap we accumulate, the more weighed-down we become. It also leads to more stuff we will have to worry about disposing of or storing in the future. It's no coincidence that the self-storage industry is booming. As Daniel Pink, author of *A Whole New Mind* points out:

"Self-storage – a business devoted to providing people a place to house their extra stuff – has become a 17 billion annual industry in the United States, larger than the motion picture business…When we can't store our many things, we just throw them away. As business writer Polly LaBarre notes, 'The United States spends more on trash bags than ninety other countries spend on everything. In other words, the receptacles of our waste cost more than all of the goods consumed by nearly half of the world's nations.'"

Better make sure you register for a sturdy trash bin. Pink also notes:

"Abundance has brought beautiful things to our lives, but that bevy of material goods has not necessarily made us much happier. The paradox of prosperity is that while living standards have risen steadily decade after decade, personal, family, and life satisfaction haven't budged. That's why more people – liberated by prosperity but not fulfilled by it – are resolving the paradox by searching for meaning."

Consume experiences, not things. Think outside the Bed Bath and Beyond box. Maybe you'll find that you don't need a slew of kitchen items, but you and your husband want a honeymoon filled with experiences. It's not uncommon to register for excursions for your honeymoon, such as parasailing, windsurfing or snorkeling. These items will enrich your life and stay with you forever, long after your silverware tarnishes and your china pattern is discontinued.

Thankfully, there are now better options for brides who wish to register in a non-traditional manner. People are catching on to the fact that our needs and styles vary greatly, and maybe we don't want our kitchens and bathrooms to look as though Crate & Barrel and Martha Stewart held hands and puked all over them. A great (and fairly new) resource to organize your registry and allow yourself to pick and choose from different places is a site called Whimventory (http://www.whimventory.com). This site is awesome because it allows you to direct your guests to one destination where they can choose among several options.

Another idea is to use your bridal shower as a means to do good for yourself and for others. Instead of playing Bridal Bingo for the bajillionth time and winning the uber-coveted re-gifted liquid hand soap, or enduring a two-hour present opening session ("Ohhhh, a toaster! [gasp] How did you know?!"), you could opt to do something a little more meaningful.

Do you like to garden, or want to start one? Throw a "garden party" in place of your shower. This is great for "green" brides, and if you're a bride who loves to cook, ask friends and family to celebrate with you by helping you plant a culinary herb garden at your home.

Maybe you're not an earth muffin, you hate cooking, and you really have no dishes to eat on. That's fine. Register for what you need, but maybe let people know from your invitation to forego the gift wrap on your presents. Even the least eco-conscious of us realize all the waste that goes into the wrapping paper from bridal shower presents, and the most ironic thing is that in many cases, for large showers, the bride doesn't even touch the paper – instead, the bridesmaids rip it off in a mad dash to keep the factory line moving and get the process over with. Take a look at a friend or relative's bridal shower pictures. Chances are you may spot a few giant black garbage bags in the background, filled with unnecessary waste. It's a pretty sad sight. It can be prevented if we all take notice and make a few adjustments.

Other non-traditional "showers" and party ideas

Stock the Bar Party: This is an excellent type of party to have once you have moved into a new space. Rather than a traditional bridal shower or housewarming, where people are often torn as to what to bring you, send out a "stock the bar" invite and get the party started. (If you are a wino, naturally, have a stock the wine fridge party.) If you decide to throw this party, have these items on hand:

*jar of simple syrup
*bag of liquor pourers
*wine glass markers (purchase or make your own)
*bag of lemons and limes
*bar tools set, including opener, jigger, strainer, shaker

It doesn't need to be anything fancy. The idea is to make it simple and easy, and to use what you have. If you have a double sink, plug one side and fill it up with ice from a bag. As your guests come, pop off the caps of their bottles and ice them. If you do not have a double sink, a large bowl filled with ice can work just as well.

Sextoy/lingerie Party: This one is not necessarily original, but it can be a lot of fun. Choose a Saturday night, get all your besties and fun friends together, and let loose.

Spa Party: A spa party can be a great way to relax and unwind before your big day. Get an idea for pricing at a local spa; if you are on a budget, your house can double just as well. Heat up damp towels with mint, lavender or rosemary in the microwave, print out some simple recipes for face masks, light some candles, and slice up some cucumbers and toss them in pitchers of water. You could even search online for a freelance nail tech to come in to give everyone a pedicure. If you don't need much off of a registry other than bath items, go ahead and register for your towels and other bath accessories, as this will complement the spa theme.

Ugly Bridesmaids Dress Party (or just plain Bridesmaids Dress Party): Invite your favorite girls over for dinner and drinks, on the premise that they wear a bridesmaid dress from the past. It doesn't necessarily need to be ugly – but of course, it's funnier if it is. If you don't have a dress to wear, a prom dress or other ugly dress will work just fine. Stay in and drink as you cut, glue and bedazzle the shit out of them, then have a runway-style "walk off." Or rent a party bus and go out on the town as a "bridal party." This has the potential to be fucking hysterical, and if I could go back and do it again, I most definitely would.

Wish for a Cause

In many areas, it is traditional to have what is called a "wishing well" at a bridal shower. If you're not familiar, it may be indicated on the shower invitation that guests should bring small, inexpensive and mostly useless items for the bride, and place them in what literally looks like a well. An extra serving spoon, a silly kitchen timer, or other unnecessary junk usually make their way in. My sister had a wishing well at her shower, and among the chotchkies inside, she found a book, wrapped, with a note on the inside cover: "Dear Deborah. I hope you enjoy this book, it made me think of you." Cute, right? Too bad my sister's name is Lisa. Apparently Deborah never cracked that sucker open before she re-gifted it to my sister by tossing it into the wishing well.

Instead of doing away with the wishing well altogether, why not ask for particular items that guests can donate? Maybe you are an animal lover. Use the opportunity for the wishing well to ask guests to bring an item for a pet, such as blankets and chew toys, and after your shower, donate the items to your favorite shelter. Maybe use it for canned food that you will donate to your local food bank. If you use your wedding as an opportunity to help others, you can do good and feel good, while simultaneously encouraging others to do the same. The end result is a positive and helpful experience – and hopefully, a more clutter-free and organized kitchen.

We are living in a time when we can no longer walk through a department store and pick out whatever our heart desires without thinking of (or being affected by) where it came from, how much wasted energy it took to make it, how many miles it was shipped, and how much of our resources were destroyed so it can sit, ever so daintily, in our china closets for years to come. If we are having children, we will be leaving these problems for them to clean up. We can vote all we want, but really the biggest way to affect change is to vote with our dollars and drop the tired trends. If we start asking for types of products, or for companies to become more responsible, and purchase those products, the change will occur.

Some honest and uncensored thoughts from a real bride regarding the bridal shower:

"If it were up to me, bridal showers would be done very different. The shower itself would be about spending time with your friends and family before your special day, catching up with them, and chatting with them about their marital experiences. It would be about laughing, and food, and wine, and the start of the bride's new life. Gifts would be left at the side of the

room for the bride to open when she got home. And guests would be happy to receive an invitation to one instead of the dread that ensues the moment one is received!

And don't get me started on the games…" ~Stacey

Bridesmaids: your role in the shower

There are many approaches to planning a bridal shower. Sometimes the mother of the bride takes a back seat and expects the girls to throw the shower; other times, the mother of the bride goes full steam ahead and plans everything on her own. I think there's a happy medium on which we can all agree, and it can be done without breaking the bank.

The shower is yet another aspect of a wedding that is totally shaped by the dynamics of a bride's family and friends, so these guidelines are by no means strict. What works in your family may not work in mine, and vice versa. But given the number of showers in which I've been involved, directly or indirectly, they have all operated in a somewhat similar fashion.

For starters, the mother of the bride normally has an idea of a place and time she'd like for her daughter's shower to be held. The maid of honor should contact the mother of the bride to get a feel for how her plans are going, and to see what kind of help she needs, and then in turn she should relay the information to the bridesmaids.

Finances are a touchy subject. The mother of the bride may or may not need help financially, but it's uncomfortable for many moms to come out and ask this of her daughter's bridesmaids. And bridesmaids have a ton of other expenses to worry about, not only for things such as the dresses, shoes, gifts, makeup, etc., but also because they may be in multiple weddings around the same time (or planning their own wedding). Not to mention mortgages, babies, and other life expenses for which they need to account.

If you are the maid of honor, I would suggest (if you can) saving a bit from when you are asked and offering to cover one or two of the shower expenses, such as the invitations, the favors, or the centerpieces. If you really are strapped financially, it's okay – don't forget that your time is just as helpful. Maybe offer to help the bride's mom send invitations, set up the room, wrap favors, or print a few of the dreaded shower games (and I beg you, if this is what you help with, please find some creative ones). This type of approach, I have found, works best, because you can be designated a single task that you can focus on and do on your own time. Ask what needs to be done, and offer what you can.

The same rule applies for bridesmaids. Offer to pick up a small tab (maybe a few of you can go in together), or offer your time to help plan or set up. Just do something to show you care and want to be involved. Communication comes into play here. Don't just do the old, "Let me know if you need anything!" email just so you can say you offered. Sure, you can get away with it, but it's too casual, and most people are not going to respond with, "Thanks, I need (a) (b) and (c)." Remember, it's not easy for many people to ask for help as they may not want to impose. Instead, ask, "What can I do to help?" And maybe check in a couple of times leading up to the shower, as things always come up last minute.

However, be mindful of coming on too strong. Sincerely offer your help once or twice, but if you receive pushback, let it go. Some women are just plain glory hogs and/or control freaks and will do everything they can to claim the shower as "theirs," with the exception of lifting their little legs and peeing on it. If no one is biting on your offers, drop it. You don't want to step on any toes.

If you are the maid of honor for a large bridal party and are trying to set a date for the shower or bachelorette party, understand that you cannot accommodate everyone. This does not mean you shouldn't at least try, however. You may not be able to stomach the bride's bratty cousin, but she's still a bridesmaid, and you need to be fair. Start by sending a blast email with two or three dates in mind. Then, sit back and wait to receive forty-five different scheduling conflicts and opinions. It's good to ask everyone to at least give the heads up, but the chances of everyone agreeing on a particular date or idea can be slim, especially if travel is involved. Choose the day that works best for most and move on.

Bridesmaids and maids of honor, one final note: Don't vent to the bride about the drama going on in terms of other bridesmaids and planning. She's got enough to worry about, so for her sake, keep the antics under wraps. Some brides may dig for information along the way and want to know the gossip, but don't say it until after the wedding – if at all.

Back to the Dais: Date Night

It's that time again to grab your hubby's hand and head back to the dais for a bit.

While planning my wedding, I ran into an acquaintance, the mother of one of my brother's childhood friends. She asked how I was doing, and we got on the topic of marriage. She leaned in and said, "Can I offer you some advice?" I felt like saying, "Go right ahead, lady, everyone else is!"

But what came next has always stuck with me. She said, "My husband and I have been married for over thirty years. One of the reasons I think we have such a wonderful relationship is because we have a "date night" every Wednesday night. We've done it since the beginning, and we still do it today." I realized just how important her advice was (while simultaneously picking the puddle of my melted self up off the floor and restraining from freaking her out by giving her a hug.)

A date night is a concept that sounds so simple. But when you break it down and think about it, with our schedules being taken over by, well, LIFE, it takes more dedication and commitment than it may seem. Our daily routines, consisting of the usual work-home-gym-dinner-bed-repeat, (minus the gym, of course), leave tiny windows of precious time for other activities: spending time with extended family and friends, partaking in hobbies, having sex, and vegging on the couch while indulging in our favorite shows. Of course you are connecting with your spouse if you are having sex, but making it a point to have a date night forces you to connect in another way that will nourish your marriage.

You don't need to break the bank in order to follow the date night ritual. Of course, getting hooched-up and going out to a fancy restaurant or for a night on the town is fun, but that's not the sort of date night I'm talking about (and I'm pretty sure this woman wasn't, either). A date night can literally consist of going into your backyard for an hour on a Tuesday night with two beach chairs, a bottle of wine and a small plate of cheese, leaving your cell phones in the house. It doesn't need to be fancy or complicated – in fact, the simpler, the better.

Here are some ideas for easy and convenient date nights (or mornings):

*Fill a travel mug with some wine or beer, and take a stroll around your neighborhood with your honey at dusk.

*Go see a movie you wouldn't normally see, then come home and talk about it over dinner. Did you like it? Did you learn something new?

*Go for a bike ride together to a new coffee or ice cream shop.

*For ballsy couples: Go to a karaoke bar in another town and perform a duet together.

*Grab a blanket, fill a basket with snacks and drinks, and head to a local park.

*Volunteer your time at an animal shelter, a fundraiser, or any other non-profit.

*Get up early and watch the sun rise together. Your day looks different when you do this.

*Do a simple DIY project together. You don't need to be pros – it can be as easy as making a photo collage of your past vacations, or painting a wall.

*Hit up a local farmers market. Purchase a fruit or vegetable you've never tried, Google a simple recipe, and make a meal together.

Here are some other fun date night ideas, collected from various sources:

*"Draw sketches of one another. Even if you can't draw, you'll have fun and create a lovely memory." ~About.com

*"Have a dance party in your living room and dance to your favorite songs from high school." ~smallnotebook.org

*"Carry along a loaf of bread and feed the ducks at the lake." ~smallnotebook.org

*"Explore unique conversation starters, such as: 'What's the habit you're proudest of breaking?' or 'If you had to be named after one of the fifty states, which would it be?' or 'What's your favorite infomercial?' ~suite101.com

*Dollar Store Extravaganza: "Just make a small budget of $10 or less and challenge each other to a contest to see who can come up with the most creative gift from the dollar store for each other." ~momadvice.com

No matter what you do together, the take-away here is to make it a point to do *something*. Make it your ritual, make it fun, make it simple, but most importantly, make it happen. It's the little things that make the big things all the better.

Table #11:
Etiquette, and the
Etiquette-less

When it comes to your wedding, you need to be prepared for everything. People will ask you things and do things that you couldn't make up if you tried. People will text you the morning of your wedding as you are getting ready, asking you for directions because they lost their invitation. A guest will call you relentlessly in the weeks leading up to your wedding, trying to get you to allow them to bring a guest (even though your budget does not allow you to do so). As you stand there positively glowing in your wedding dress, people may complain to you that their food is too cold, that the band is too loud, or that they don't like their table. Oh yes. They walk among us.

As my new husband and I were walking around saying hello to the guests at our reception, someone scribbled out a check and tried to hand it to me, loose, with no card. Woohoo! Thanks, sweet cheeks! Should I tuck it in my cleavage, along with the singles I collected from table number five? She apologized for not having a card or envelope to put it in, but said she'd surely get one and mail it to me. I told her not to worry, to just hang on to the check and send it with the card – no big deal. The person in question spent the next hour at her table loudly fighting with her husband, before storming out and leaving him behind at our wedding. I never did receive that card. But hey, guess what? No harm, no foul. I don't care if that check had an amount of $1,000 written on it. If it meant someone with that little amount of class leaving my wedding, I'll gladly give up the money.

When it comes to guest etiquette, you just…don't…know.

Guest Etiquette You May Encounter

*RSVPs (or lack thereof.) As a bride, nothing is more frustrating than waiting for Aunt Jeannie to get her shit together and pop that sucker in the mail. Count on the fact that you'll have a few Aunt Jeannies. As frustrating as it is, sometimes people lose the RSVP under a stack of bills (those envelopes are usually small and easy to misplace), or they simply just forget to respond in time. Go down your list and see if the slackers are on your side or your future spouse's. Then ask either your mom or your groom's mom if they could ~~smack them upside their head~~ gently relay the message to the guest in question to check the appropriate box and fork it on over, so no one gets hurt.

*People who may call you regarding their "plus one." People should never assume they can bring a guest to a wedding unless the words "and guest" are written next to their name on the invitation, but don't put it past anyone to call you and beg. While I'm sure they're upset that they can't bring their new biffy, you and your groom are probably on a strict budget and had to trim your list. As rude as it may be to put you on the spot, try not to get offended when asked. Gently let the guest know that they are not singled out here. If you make an exception for them, you will feel the wrath from others who were invited solo. Unless the "plus one" is a seeing-eye dog for a special needs guest, stick to your guns on this one.

*Guests who will disrupt your ceremony. Cell phones blaring and latecomers are often the biggest cause for disruption during your ceremony.

Nothing is more awkward than a latecomer who barrels through the church doors right before the bride – or worse, right behind her. Don't stress about it if it happens. Just block it out and keep your attention on your husband and your ceremony, and everyone else will follow your lead.

*People who try to corner you at your reception**. While guests want to wish you well and catch up, there is a fine line between chit-chat and cornering. It's a busy day and you are being pulled in several different directions, and if you have a large amount of guests at your wedding, you will wear yourself out trying to catch up with all of them. Don't beat yourself up over this. You may have the best of intentions, but if you shoot the shit for too long you may spend the first half of your wedding saying "hello", and the second half saying "goodbye." Catch up with them with some one-on-one time after the wedding is over.

And for the love of god, I hope no guests gripe to you about the tiny bathroom stalls, the poor directions, or the shitty weather, but sometimes it happens. The day of our wedding was a non-stop torrential downpour, but honestly, we couldn't have cared less – we were too busy to notice, and we were having a great time. But a good amount of people felt the need to bring up to us how "terrible" the weather was, and how it was "good luck" for the marriage. I know they meant well, but we didn't need to be reminded of the doom and gloom outside. Tell me it's good luck if a bird shits on my head as I'm entering the church - because at that point, I'll need your condolences. But really, you can't do anything about the weather, and during that day, you'll probably already be over it. Your guests should be, too.

*Some woman who may wear white to your wedding**. You can probably count on the fact that no one will wear white to your wedding. But sometimes, it happens. However, in all honesty, who really cares? You are the bride, and no one will "upstage" you, so just relax and have fun.

*A guest who lugs a bulky gift to your wedding**. It may be tempting to wish for that 900-pound stand mixer you have been coveting, but let's hope no one brings it to your wedding. Because if a guest is lugging that sucker in, that means you and your groom have to lug it out. Hopefully they stick to something small and manageable (cash in a card, anyone?) and if they do purchase a bulky gift off of the registry, they are savvy enough have it sent directly to your home.

*Unsigned cards, and free-floating gifts.** We received mostly cards with money for our wedding, but there was that one pretty basket with a nice bottle of red wine, a nice bottle of white wine, two pretty blue glasses and a picture frame. To this day, we have no idea who gave it to us because there was no card attached. We also received an envelope with $200 in it – with no message or signature. These were nice gestures, but since we were unable to identify who gave these gifts, we could never properly thank them. If this happens to you, run down your guest list to narrow it down to a select few suspects. (Side note: when you open your cards and gifts, do yourself a favor and create a spreadsheet to record the gifts you received and who they were from. My mom gave me this advice, which I at first thought was unnecessary, but I can't tell you how many times I have referenced it when determining how much to give to others for weddings and special events. It may sound tacky at first, but it is helpful. If someone gave us $300 for our wedding, I want to make sure I don't short-change them when it's their time to say "I do.")

Bride Etiquette

One of the most common threads in this book is *balance*. No matter what goes on in your wedding planning, striking a healthy balance can be a struggle – but it is extremely rewarding in the long run. It can be especially difficult to determine proper etiquette during wedding planning, so here are a few common situations, and some solutions to deal with them:

*Word your invitation properly.** Yikes. This one can be a toughie because of finances. There are many options here depending on who's investing in your big day. For example, if both sets of parents will be contributing, you could say:

Mr. and Mrs. So-and-So,
And
Mr. and Mrs. Blah-Blah-Blah,
Request the honor of your presence
At the
Marriage of their children…

If only your parents are contributing, but you still want to mention your groom's parents, you may say:

Mr. and Mrs. So-and-So
Request the honor of your presence at the marriage of their daughter,
Little-Miss-Thing,
To
Big-Daddy,
Son of
Mr. and Mrs. Blah-Blah-Blah…

Do whatever you like, but I suggest you make the effort to honor both sets of parents by including their names on the invitation, even if they aren't contributing. Maybe your hubby's parents are not your favorite people, but remember: If it weren't for that fateful, drunken night when his dad turned up the charm and took his mom home to dance the horizontal mambo, your man would not be here to begin with.

***Don't make anyone feel left out**. Be sure to include your mother, mother-in-law, grandmother, or whoever else you are close to in some part of your wedding. Honoring them, even with the smallest gesture, will make them feel involved and special. Maybe your crazy mother-in-law, or your overbearing Aunt Betty, aren't your favorite people, but giving them something they can own will make them feel good, and keep them off your back (even if just for a few minutes). Plus, keeping them busy will give them less time to perform any antics.

***Be polite**. When talking about your wedding, almost everyone will have an opinion for you. While some are welcome, the bulk will not be, and this can be very, very irritating. It may be tempting to follow through with your visions of drop-kicking them off of your guest list, but instead, prepare yourself with a general answer that will shut them the eff up. When you receive unsolicited "advice", try one of these:

The *"thanks but no thanks" approach*: "Thanks! I love that you are thinking of me." Then redirect the conversation.

The *"catch them off-guard and make them walk away" approach*: "Great idea! Hey, come closer for a second - do I need to wax my stache?"

The *"I hear ya!" approach*: "Hey, cool! Thanks! I'm still tossing some ideas around, so I'll take it into consideration."

The *"lips are sealed" approach*: If you have someone that is really annoying and won't stop badgering you for details, give them the ol' "Everything is a surprise!" answer. This shuts them down from the beginning and they will likely get the hint that you don't want to discuss anything with them.

Whichever option you choose, politely excuse yourself from the conversation when you are done and keep it moving (except for the "catch them off-guard" approach, in which case usually takes care of itself). Whatever you do, DO NOT attempt to justify what you are doing to naysayers, or spill any details to known copy-cats. It's not worth your precious energy and you will kick yourself later. Remember…

"Opinions are like assholes; everyone has one." ~Author Unknown

***Express gratitude**. If your future in-laws are chipping in for your big day, acknowledge this and thank them right away. It doesn't matter how, but the point is to show your gratitude and let them know you appreciate them chipping in. It doesn't need to be anything fancy – send a greeting card, or take them out for a light brunch if your funds will allow for it. Just make the gesture, and get your relationship off on the right foot.

***Write a nice thank you card**. It's very time-consuming to write two-hundred "thank you" cards, but I recommend you suck it up and just do it. Many brides sidestep this by sending out a nice picture and generic message to all who attended their big day. You can certainly get away with this, and there's nothing really *wrong* with it, but I would suggest you opt to write a special message to each guest. It's a nice touch to personally acknowledge your guests for sharing your day and giving you a gift. At the very least, send the generic photo card and message to most guests, but write a heartfelt "thanks" to those closest to you who went the extra mile. Grab a bottle of wine, block off a free Saturday or Sunday, and knock it out. You can bill them for your carpel tunnel later.

Table #12: Your Mental Health

Do you, reader, take yourself, to have and to hold?

The relationship we maintain with ourselves is the most important relationship we can have, and it sets the tone for every other bond in our lives. This isn't meant to be cliché or to sound like a Hallmark card. It is a simple truth. You must love yourself and nourish your soul before you can fully offer yourself to another.

And in order to do this, on occasion, you must bitch-slap yourself. Just like a diamond, we bitches are multi-faceted. Our moods can change (especially when Aunt Flow swings by for a visit), and it's up to us to keep ourselves in check.

You know that out-of-control child you have met? The one who walks all over his parents because they do not discipline him? It's obvious he is in need of some serious tough love from Mom and Dad. He may hate his parents at first, but in the end, he will respect them for the life lessons they instilled. In most cases, if the crazy behavior is left unchecked, it will only worsen – and may even result in him resenting his parents down the road. Discipline is not easy, but the payoff far outweighs the work involved.

Sometimes, *we* are the adult version of that child. But the beauty of being a grown-up is that we are also the parent. It's natural that the child within us will sometimes act out of control. But as long as we call upon that inner parent to swoop in with a swift bitch-slap, we can continue to be the best version of ourselves to our spouse, and everyone else in our lives.

Let's get back to our unfortunate virus. There will come a time during your wedding planning where you may surprise yourself by showing symptoms of cRzybTch1. You'll be sitting there making a decision about a cake, or a dress fitting or what have you, and suddenly your mouth will open and you will say something along the lines of: "It's all about ME today," or "I don't care – I want it that way and I will get my way," or maybe it's, "That bitch better lose ten pounds before being in pictures on MY wedding day."

Upon this occurrence, promptly excuse yourself for a moment. Go into the bathroom, enter a stall, and lock the door. Then raise your right hand, open up your palm, and bitch-slap yourself. You are not this person, nor will you become her.

On the other side of the spectrum (but equally as detrimental): If you find yourself being walked all over by others, or dipping into savings accounts and being pressured into spending money you don't have, you still must enter that bathroom stall and take care of business. Yes, it is of course your day, and yes, you should honor your wishes and throw the wedding you envisioned. A wedding is a big life event and you should enjoy it. But there is a fine line between sipping the Kool-Aid ever so gently, lips pursed and pinky up, versus pouring the shit all over your head. Being a bride doesn't give you a free pass to be a diva – or a doormat. Strike that blissful balance in between. Here's a good place to start:

*If you find yourself stomping your feet like a child and uttering the phrase "I can act like this, because it's MY day!" **you must bitch-slap yourself**.

*If you find yourself being trampled on by others or affected by haters, **you must bitch-slap yourself**.

*If you find yourself making demands and talking down to brides-maids, family members or your soon-to-be groom, **you must bitch-slap yourself**.

*If you find yourself flipping out on your fiancé when he needs a break from wedding planning, **you must bitch-slap yourself**.

*If you aren't enjoying this special time in your life because you are becoming too stressed or worried about this four-hour event that will be over faster than you can say "I do," **you must bitch-slap yourself**.

*If you are depriving your body of proper nutrients and abusing it with treacherous workouts or tanning bed "sunburns," **you must bitch-slap yourself**.

*If you are maxing out credit cards and driving yourself into debt to have the best of the best in everything, **you must bitch-slap yourself**.

The goal is to take care of yourself, both mentally and physically, and to not to cross over into Crazytown and obsess over things that really aren't helping you in the long run.

One of my favorite books that I read and re-read to put myself in check is called *Life's Too F***ing Short*, by Janet Street-Porter. It's a fun book, an easy read, and makes a hell of a lot of sense when you find yourself in stress mode. While it pertains to life in general, it can certainly be applied to wedding planning. The following excerpt is a gem:

> "We are assaulted with advice on every side, from fashion and beauty writers to 'tips' from celebrities. Newspapers and magazines now give a large amount of space, not just to advice columnists, but also to 'life' gurus, and advisers who lecture us on everything from diet to ethical living. The end result, after reading the Saturday or Sunday papers, with all their supplements, is utter exhaustion and a sense of confusion and inadequacy. A huge industry has grown up that purports to 'help' women, but in my opinion just does the complete opposite."

She goes on to recite my favorite list:

> "When you wake up, lie still for two minutes. Recite over and over again: 'I am bloody brilliant. I am great. I am number one. Unique. I like me. I am worth it. I am highly intelligent, no matter what others may say.' You have to do this, because, take it from me, no one else is ever going to tell you that in the coming twenty-four hours. To value myself is the single most important thing I have learned over the years."

The trick to bitch-slapping is to step outside of yourself for a moment and admit that you are acting in a way that may not be best for you or those you love. This takes guts, but we are all human, and we all act out at one point or another. We are both the devil and the angel that sits on our shoulders. Making mistakes is how we learn and grow. But if we refuse to see them, if we refuse to acknowledge our behavior, it will worsen, and our relationships will inevitably suffer. We make choices at every point in our lives as to what side of ourselves we will nurture, and these decisions ultimately shape who we are. I always remind myself of this story I heard several years ago:

One evening an old Cherokee told his grandson about a battle that goes on inside people.

He said, "My son, the battle is between two wolves inside us all.

One is Evil. It is anger, envy, jealousy, sorrow, regret, greed, arrogance, self-pity, guilt, resentment, inferiority, lies, false pride, superiority, and ego.

The other is Good. It is joy, peace, love, hope, serenity, humility, kindness, benevolence, empathy, generosity, truth, compassion and faith."

The grandson thought about it for a minute and then asked his grandfather: "Which wolf wins?"

The old Cherokee simply replied, "The one you feed."

Of all the guests at your wedding that you save a plate for, please be sure you do not feed the first wolf.

Bitch-slapping yourself for someone else's actions

In some instances, you may find that you are not the person who acted out, but instead, it is someone close to you. While it may be tempting, you probably shouldn't drag them into a bathroom stall and bitch-slap them. But you *can* try your best to make sure you are not affected by someone else's crappy actions. In short, this means letting things go.

"Holding a grudge & harboring anger/resentment is poison to the soul. Get even with people...but not those who have hurt us; forget them. Instead get even with those who have helped us." ~Steve Maraboli, acclaimed business trainer, speaker

Maraboli makes an excellent point. Instead of focusing on how someone has wronged us, we'd be much better off forgetting them and thinking about those who have done us right. As human beings we have only a certain amount of energy, and for every bit of it that is given to a negative thought or action, some is being taken away from something positive. Sometimes we need to evaluate how much time we spend with a negative person, or thinking about what a negative person has done to us, because this depletes our own energy reserves.

Notification: Your Energy Account Has Been Overdrafted

Ever have the kind of day where you face-plant in your bed at night, feeling totally spent? Maybe you overextended yourself at work, maybe you spent a lot of time worrying or agonizing over something that upset you, or maybe you have been going out of your mind trying to accommodate everyone as you plan your wedding. Maybe you had an all-out vent-fest over something that's been bothering you, or maybe you allowed someone to vent to you for a while. No matter what the instance was, one thing is for sure: you invested emotional energy, and you've exhausted your funds.

We are emotional beings, no matter how much or how little, and it's hard not to let things get to us. Sure, it's fine to put your emotional energy into your wedding, or get angry about things once in a while – therapeutic, even. It's great to want to devote your time and energy into helping someone and lending an ear. But remember that every bit of energy you give out is energy you lose, and that the supply is not endless. As you worry about your budget during your planning and your financial spending, remember to pay attention to your emotional spending as well – especially the *negative* emotional spending. This will do a great deal of help for your mental wallet.

Think about it: you wouldn't walk down the street and hand money to anyone in your path who asks for it, would you? It's your hard earned money. Maybe you'll pop into a few stores and make a purchase, maybe you'll spare some change for someone in need. But you only have X amount of dollars, and you can't spend it all or you'll be broke. You can't treat your account as if there is no bottom. So why would you treat your emotions that way?

Budget Yourself

There are several things that go on inside our bodies when we get upset, and you don't need a scientific degree to understand that these feelings affect us down to our core. Because of this, we have to protect ourselves. If a friend asks you for money that you don't have, you would simply let them know that you'd love to help them, but you just don't have the money. Take the same approach with your emotional dollars. If you are around someone who is an emotional vampire, constantly sucking your energy into a negative tailspin, don't be afraid to put your hand up and tell them your wallet is empty. Devoting too much emotional spending on negative people and thoughts is the quickest way to find yourself broke and homeless. Track your emotional expenses the same way you'd track your bills.

Spend your emotional money on the good stuff: great friends, positive experiences, and bettering yourself. Make "joy" your emotional money tree. Joy is like an investment: the more you allow yourself to feel it, the more you want to spread it, the more you get even more back. You know that expression, "You have to spend money to earn money"? Well, you have to spend joy in order to earn joy. Once you see the worth of this tactic and tap into it, you'll be unstoppable. Suddenly, you'll be the Oprah Winfrey of emotional money, shelling out all of your joy to share with the world. "YOU get some joy, YOU get some joy, and YOU get some joy!" It's inevitable that sometimes we will find ourselves in the red, but for the most part, with this mentality we'll see our joy profits skyrocket well into the black.

In the end, when it comes to your wedding planning, you can spend your emotional money any way you want to – just remember to pay attention to what you're buying, and be sure not to deplete your funds.

Social Vampires

You know those people who can't function a day in their lives without being told or reminding the world every five minutes just how fucking fabulous they are? The "me-me's" and Narcy Darcys who are only in it for the self-gain, who cut you off every time you go to speak and freak out every time the spotlight is removed from them? They subject anyone who will listen to unending self-talk and/or pompous status updates and their relationships are often one-way streets.

Listen to me closely: RUN from these people. They are social vampires. They will suck you dry of all of your energy and leave you feeling zapped and spent after every encounter you have with them. They don't care about your well-being and never will. If you have a social vampire in your life, it is time to limit their access to your world. This doesn't have to involve a big blowout, or any other bitter feelings. Just simply phase them out, little by little, and avoid as much drama as possible.

If a social vampire resides inside the walls of your own family, well, then things get a bit trickier. That's not to say you can't fix the problem. You just need to distance yourself and tune them out. I like to refer to these people as type "OO," which is short for "output only" – they are not equipped to input and process any information. This is all fine for them, but it doesn't mean that you need to be the dumping ground for this person's every thought and emotion. There comes a point where you need to preserve your precious time and energy, and trust me – during wedding planning, you need to reserve every piece of time and energy you can.

Your Multiple Personalities

Who was that crazy bitch in the bridal salon who had a breakdown over not finding the perfect gown? What about the one who freaked out on her bridesmaid because of the innocent little question she asked about the reception? Or the one who went full-out APE SHIT on her fiancé for suggesting they do something – anything – on Friday night other than talk about or plan the wedding? That wasn't you. That was Psycho Suzy, Crazy Carrie and Nutjob Nancy, but no, definitely not you. If any of these whack-jobs decide to crash your wedding, designate a table for them. Maybe in the coatroom. With a straight-jacket and a padlock.

Weddings are emotional and sometimes these crazy characters emerge out of us due to sheer stress. It's your wedding, the big day, your moment, the time where everything must be perfect. Photos will be taken, video will be rolling, drinks will be flowing, and all will be capped by a fabulous honeymoon that will send you off into the sunset of "Forever After." It's all peaches and candy. But in all honesty, it's important to realize that no matter how much you plan or stress over your wedding, it will not be perfect. It can't be, because that's just life. Whether big or small, you will never get it

100-percent right. That is, of course, unless you go into it with the mindset that *something will go wrong,* and that *it's okay.*

Imperfection Makes Perfect a Wedding: Rula's Story

"For our wedding day my (then) fiancé and I booked a beautiful venue in Charlotte, NC, a large Inn surrounded by a beautiful landscape maintained with lovely gardens. Our wedding was held outdoors on September 6, 2003 and the weather turned out to be absolutely perfect. The sun was shining and the breeze was soft and cool as we said our 'I do's' under a white arbor nestled between two gardens. The solo violinist didn't seem to miss a single note or key and everything from the procession of bridesmaids and groomsmen, to the walk of sweet little flower girls, to the lighting of the candles went smoothly all while the photographer proactively clicked away at his camera. After our nuptials, dinner was served outside beneath a large tent lined with lights. My husband and I were formally introduced as 'Mr. and Mrs. Shin' as we walked into the magical dinner setting under a shower of exuberant applause and whistles, feeling like a king and queen! Family and friends had not only come from all over the country to attend our wedding, but from all over the world! We felt so lucky and so happy that so many of our loved ones were able to share our day with us.

The meal was delicious and the cutting of the cake and the speeches given by the maid of honor and best man were sentimental and heartwarming. After everyone had dinner and cake, we all went indoors to the Inn's large ballroom to attend the wedding reception. The music was played by a deejay that we hired. He did a good job playing from a list of American genres that we requested, as well as playing Arabic music that we had provided him. The party was well on its way and everyone drank and danced their hearts away into the night!

Now, this Inn has a honeymoon suite which we had booked for the evening along with several rooms for the wedding party. Our flight to Hawaii was not until early the next morning. So, our plan was to signal the end of the reception by telling the deejay to announce our so called departure from the Inn to leave for our honeymoon, and that everyone should gather outside to wish us farewell by showering us with the bubbles they had all been given earlier in the day. The deejay seemed to understand this plan and was happy to oblige, and as the night was nearing an end we realized that the entire day and evening had basically gone off without a hitch! Well, almost. The night, it seems, was still a bit young.

Sometime between 11:30 and midnight it was decided that my husband and I would make our false exit out of the Inn to signal the end of the reception. As we prepared ourselves for the walk out of the Inn, the manager of the Inn went to the deejay and whispered into his ear, 'Okay, it's now time for the bride and groom's fake exit. Please tell everyone to gather outside with their bubbles to wish them farewell and good luck.' 'Sounds good,' he replied. The manager then came back and told us to get ready at the top of the stairs as everyone would be outside eagerly awaiting our descent and exit, after which we would sneak back into the Inn from a back door and settle ourselves into the honeymoon suite.

My husband and I were beaming. I was so tired and the entire evening seemed like a kind of whirlwind dream to me, but I was so happy and eager to retire to our honeymoon suite. As we stood at the top of the stairs we listened for the deejay's announcement which was our cue to start walking down the spiral staircase. Soon after, we heard the music stop and the deejay get on the microphone. 'Excuse me everybody! May I please have your attention! I would like to make an announcement. Will everyone please gather the bubbles that were given to you earlier in the day and make your way towards the back door in preparation for the bride and groom's FAKE exit. Thank you.' Yes. You heard right. He said, 'fake exit.' My husband and I just looked at each other for a few seconds in disbelief and then suddenly burst out laughing! We could see the confusion on people's faces in the crowd below and all the whisperings of 'fake wha..? What's going on?'

Well...so much for perfection. But you know what? The entire wedding truly was perfection, 'fake exit' or not. In fact, it was this tiny and hilarious 'imperfection' which truly gave our wedding its unique personality, lending the occasion an image of personalized perfection! Without this little incident the wedding would have gone a little too smoothly, and then what colorful story would we have come away with to tell our children and grandchildren? This 'flaw' turned out to be the best 'grand finale' we could have asked for, bringing to a close an impression of this magical evening that will forever remain imprinted in my heart's memory.' ~Rula

The lesson: the only thing you need to make a perfect wedding is you and your hubby.

Another point of reference that is close to home for me is a story about what happened with my parents' wedding, as told by my mother (and try to read it to yourself in a dramatic, thick New York accent, because it's just more fun that way):

"Before the wedding, we fixed up the house with a fresh coat of paint inside and out. We bought an air conditioner (a first, remember, this was 1971) and new grass sod for the entire lawn. We purchased and planted an array of gorgeous flowers. Unfortunately there was only one thing we couldn't control: THE WEATHER! We had a hurricane the day before our wedding. It was pouring rain, and everything we had done outside was destroyed. Luckily, the next day – our wedding day – was beautiful and sunny. I climbed into the limo and my dad announced: 'I said a prayer today. I told my Pop to let Jo Ann have a beautiful day and it happened!' We made it out unscathed from the weather, but we weren't out of the woods yet - our baker had other plans...

"My future husband and I had picked out a wedding cake. We made our way to an Italian bakery in the Bronx (which shall remain nameless at this point, as it is still in business today) and chose a beautiful cake. Fast forward to the evening of our event, as the staff are about to retrieve the cake so they may cut it and serve it. But one problem arose: NO CAKE. We all thought they were kidding, but it was true. My future husband got on the phone and found out from the baker that HE THOUGHT THE EVENT WAS THE NEXT DAY. He told us he would get to the bakery and deliver us something right away. Shortly after, we were delivered a cake alright: four layers, all different sizes, plopped on top of a square sheet cake! We cut this disaster and served it, but it wasn't long before we noticed that all four cakes had different fillings, and the sheet cake was bone-dry.

"All I can leave you with are these words: whatever will be, will be. Everything falls into place. When obstacles arise, just go with the flow, because it all works out. Most importantly, remember that you are creating beautiful memories for yourself and your children, and are leaving behind legacies for generations to come, franken-cake, or no franken-cake."

Back to the Dais

"I love being married. It's so great to find that one special person you want to annoy for the rest of your life." ~Rita Rudner

It's inevitable that you will fight and annoy each other, and some of those fights will be over some heavy issues. But it's helpful and reassuring to know that a good amount of those fights will be about some pretty petty shit – silly things that you know annoy the other, or certain times that, for you or your partner, aren't good for conflict.

For us, the morning is not a good time to bring up a petty topic. This is partly because we are both in a rush to get out of the house, but also because I have not eaten anything yet. As crazy as that sounds, for me, it's simple: I am very irritable when I'm hungry. As Greg so eloquently puts it, there is a "fucking ruthless monster" living inside my stomach that will not subside until I eat something. Most of the ridiculous and petty fights Greg and I have had occurred in the morning because of said monster. So now we know, and we can act accordingly.

We have two options. The first is to avoid talking about touchy subjects early in the morning. The second involves a project that Greg is currently researching, and that is to install a toaster oven in the headboard of our bed so that when the alarm clock goes off, before I can process a thought, it automatically shoves two Pop Tarts directly into my mouth (patent pending).

If you know your honey is always stressed at work in the afternoon, try to put off a "hot button" topic until you are both home and settled. If you know that you like to unwind at night before bed and don't want to get into any in-depth conversations about finances, gently let him know that particular time is off-limits and make it a rule. Not only does this help you stop fighting, but it also creates mutual respect for one another.

Of course, fights can be sporadic, but knowing the best times to talk it out or walk away is half the battle. Save the big issues for when you are both thinking clearly. Recognize the petty shit, and the need to let it go. We may not understand why certain things annoy our spouse, or why they can't fathom how a certain thing irritates us, and that's okay. We just need to understand and acknowledge that it does, and plan accordingly.

Table #13:
Here Comes
the Groom

Let's give your groom some TLC, because let's face it: weddings are way more focused on the bride. It's all about YOUR dress, YOUR hair, and what YOU want, no matter how much or how little your man is involved in the planning process.

Most men completely understand this and are happy to hand over the spotlight. But for the purposes of this book, and for the planning of your wedding, it only seems fair that we pay him some extra attention at a time when no one else probably will.

So, I ask you to hand the book over for just a few moments to your future hubs. The following is for him and only him to read. When he's done, he can give it right back to you, but if you wouldn't mind, I'd like a moment alone with him. I promise not to show any cleavage. (You're in luck, I don't have much anyway. Ha.) Okay, now pass me on over, sister.

MEN:

I could give you a pretty straight-forward section here with a tired to-do list of the usual stuff you might hear: rent a dapper tux so you look great for your lady, don't smash cake into your bride's face, don't get too drunk at your bachelor party and show up late to the altar, blah-blah-bligetty-*blahhh*, but you're better than that. I'm giving you credit here where credit is due because grooms of today, like you, are sensitive and in-tune with their ladies, not irresponsible, bumbling frat boys. Even if you guys aren't spewing with enthusiasm for wedding planning, you know and care enough to be affected by this little circus.

I'm not going to make this section unnecessarily long or painful, either – I'm cutting right to the chase and giving you the high-level important shit you need to know. Here we go:

- Show interest in the wedding planning process. I'm not saying to cross the line and start choosing color schemes and table linens without consulting your bride, but a little display of excitement is welcome and will show her you really are the sensitive stud she wants to marry. And by "excitement," I don't mean erupting into a panic attack and freaking out when seeing the price tag of the flower arrangements and ice sculptures. If you are having a financial issue, save it for when you get home and it's just you two. We don't need to be finding you in the bread aisle of the grocery store tearing open hot dog bun packages a la Steve Martin in *Father of the Bride*.
- Help her out with your family. Wedding planning usually involves communicating with your mom, sisters, aunts, and whomever else may or may not have fallen down and forgotten that they aren't the ones getting married. If she's stressing over your side's lack of RSVP's or being swallowed whole by the demands of others, it might be time for you to (gently) step in and regulate that shit for her. Help a sister out, ya know? Blame it on yourself. Take one for your new "team". It will sound much better coming from you, where it could be received as "the adorable husband interested in wedding plan-

ning," rather than the "psycho fire-breathing bridezilla" who dares to challenge the family's opinion on napkin colors. You feel me?

- Be careful with your bride. You really are from Mars, and she really is from Venus. But there are ways to live in harmony and speak her language. We women will tell you what we need. You may need to become a bit of an investigator to decode us, but you can do it. Pay attention.
- Know that we are very patient, and you can probably push us pretty far. We are loyal. Determined to make things work. But keep in mind that you should be careful just how far you push us, because we operate differently than men. When a woman is done, she's done for good.
- Be her support system. Overall, there's no way to predict the stress you guys may both experience while planning this shindig. Chances are, however, that most of it will fall on her shoulders and the reality is that this is an emotional time for many women.

Here, some advice straight from a man who's been down this aisle before – my husband, Greg:

"You are now part of a team. You and your wife are now Co-Executive Vice Presidents of your family. She's your all-star player, your #1 draft pick. And you are hers too, dude. Your mission in this whole game of wedding planning is to keep each other grounded, to remind each other of what's important, and what you know will make the two of you most happy.

"Be involved with planning and be her sounding board, but make it your job to do one or two things together every week that don't involve planning the wedding. It might be hard for her especially to pull back from it but help her de-stress and keep your relationship at the forefront of all this, not the party.

"Also, if something is bothering you or if you aren't comfortable with the direction this wedding celebration is going, speak up. You'll want to do everything to make your bride happy, but you have to be happy, too. Remember, you guys are a team.

"One last thing: do something special for her after the ceremony that just the two of you can share together. There is so much hype and pressure surrounding the wedding ceremony and reception that no one thinks too much about the space between the last dance and the honeymoon. (Alright, well, you probably know ONE thing that you hope to happen, but that's not what I'm talking about.) No matter how much your girl loves to party, there is a glorious calm that happens after the cake is cut and you go back home, or back to your hotel room. Let me be more specific: she may love her dress, but is probably dying to get out of it because it's been cramping her ability to breathe normally for twelve hours; her hair looks beautiful, but she can't wait to rip out those bobby pins that have been poking her head all day. YOU are the one person she can kick back with and get comfortable. So, while she's in the bathroom, use those precious minutes to set something special up for her. It doesn't need to be elaborate or expensive. Play your favorite song, pour a glass of champagne for her, give a card just to tell her you love her…just something to help her *exhale*. I can't tell you what makes her or your relationship unique, but you know what it is, so figure it out and make a plan. This little romantic gesture will go a LONG way."

Got it, guys? Good. Now, a few words on the relationship…

"Happy Wife, Happy Life"

We've all heard this before, and you probably think I'm going to tell you to tattoo this onto your heart and abide by it at all times. Yes and no.

The phrase holds true for a lot of people because in many marriages, the woman is the center of the home, the emotional glue keeping everyone and everything together. While this is true in many cases, I think the phrase is a little outdated because most couples of today are a team; we need each other. And for a marriage to work, we need to *both* be happy.

I also don't like the "happy wife, happy life" mantra because it generalizes our roles in relationships, paints women as demanding, and treats men as submissive pushovers. I sort of like "happy spouse, happy life" better, although that doesn't have quite the same ring to it.

Yes, you need to pick and choose your battles, and marriage is all about sacrifice, but you also need to keep the harmony in your relationship by being comfortable with a healthy confrontation every so often.

Sometimes issues may arise, and one person doesn't want to rock the boat by calling the other out on their BS. Instead, they opt for the "keep the peace" attitude, and sweep the issue under the rug. Eventually, however, so much dust is swept under that rug that a lump forms, and before long, that lump turns into a giant mound that fills the room, the rug sitting at the top like a tiny hat. Ladies (yes, I'm talking to you again, because I know you're still reading), when necessary, if your man is acting out, speak your mind. Men, if you are being walked all over, pick up your balls and take a stand. You may think you're doing the right thing by not confronting your spouse, but in the end, you become an enabler if you let the behavior happen without addressing the situation. There is only so much sacrifice, so much overlooking, that one person can handle.

Brides: Do you really want your man to hide petty things from you, for fear that you will freak out? What happened to that cool-headed, understanding woman he married? Eventually he will snap (as would we) and, as we all know, "snapping" can come in many forms: lying, sneaking around, hiding things and possibly worse. What are we doing here? This is supposed to be the man we love, our partner, the one person with whom we are supposed to compromise, understand, and care for, just as much as we expect this from them.

The same goes for you, gentlemen: If something is going on that you are not happy about, talk it out. Don't keep it all in, or fight and explode about it and then hope it goes away, because it won't. In fact, it will come back tenfold.

Communicate, communicate, communicate – I cannot stress this enough. Without communication, your relationship is set up to fail. Even if you stay married, without communication one of you, and eventually both of you, will be unhappy and resentful, and that's not good for anyone involved. Lay it out there and talk it through. It won't be pretty. But in the end, you will be stronger for it, and you will find that you are much happier because of the time you invested in understanding each other.

Here, an excerpt from the article "Fly-By-Night Nuptials," by Sascha Rothchild for YourTango:

> "At first we complemented each other; I helped him get motivated to put down the video game controller and actually pursue an acting career, and he helped me calm down and enjoy the quiet moments between stressing out about my writing career. But after a while we both just resented the other's very different attitude, rhythm and personality. We were also so conscious of never stepping on each other's toes that we ended up compromising to the point that we were both miserable…While I was planning my 30th birthday party, I realized I didn't want my husband on the guest list…Once married, I realized that keeping the knot tied is a lot of daily work, which only just begins with 'I do.' I made the mistake, as do many women, of focusing on getting married rather than on the actual marriage."

Man, woman, husband, wife: Put your gloves on and fight. Of course, I don't mean literally beat the shit out of each other, or scream or yell like a lunatic. Just learn how to stand up for your beliefs while holding a mutual respect for your partner. This is what it takes for a successful marriage. No one has an easy marriage, not even Perfect Peggy down the road who brags about her wedded bliss every time you see her. Acknowledging problems and working through them are healthy. Don't hide under the "compromise" cloak to avoid hashing it out. Remember, you got married in the first place to have that one person who will stick by you no matter what. You owe it to each other to work at it when the going gets tough.

Of course, this doesn't mean to turn every little thing into a confrontation. You pick and choose your battles. But when it comes to the important things, don't be afraid to get your hands dirty.

Don't just take it from me. Here, the real account of Mary, a woman who divorced after fifteen years of marriage and trying to "keep the peace":

"Marriage is not about the glitz and glam. It's about love, partnership and commitment. I loved a man since I was 15 years old. I was a 'Lifer'. At the age of 39 I couldn't wait to get home to him, still had butterflies when I saw him, I wanted to do everything with him and I never asked for much just his love and affection. I swept a lot of stuff under the rug so we could remain 'happy.' Then after 17 years it all built up. I had enough, and it ended. He never communicated with me, the partnership was always one sided, he existed in a house with me and two children unhappily. I realize I was part of the problem. What I did learn, is to always love each other no matter what, have interests together and separately, and to talk, talk, talk and talk. Take the time out to be together. Make those moments count even if for a second. Always, always, always remember why you fell in love, it's the core of your relationship."

Ok, boys, you're done. This was fun. Now hand the book back to your woman before I start talking about periods and varicose veins. I mean it: I've installed new technology in this book that, when held by a man for too long, will emit a slow and steady stream of girl farts. Pass the book to your bride, and no one gets Dutch oven-ed.

Back to the Dais

Get a Life

If your idea of a hobby is waiting for your hubby to come home from his, it's time to get a life. If your hubby's idea of a hobby is crashing your "girls' nights," it's time for him to get a life. If you do not each find your own interests, you will suffocate each other.

It's cute at first how you can't wait to see each other, how you don't want them to go out, how you miss them when they are doing other things. But you need to find ways to enjoy time to yourself, and to allow your partner to do the same. And no, spying on him and shopping do not count as hobbies. I mean healthy habits, ones that encourage your personal growth. Here, a personal experience on finding what it is that interests you…

"Find Your Key in Life"

While visiting family in NY recently, I was able to go watch my dad play the saxophone at Lucy's, a local bar. My dad is an incredibly talented saxophone player, and I do not just say this because he is my father. Anyone who has seen him play can attest to this. He's been playing for pretty much his entire life, and rarely will you ever see him read music from a piece of paper. That night he was participating in a "jam session," where he brings his saxophone and just gets on stage with a group of other musicians, playing along to various songs. He does this a few times a week. The next morning we went for a walk, and as we talked about the idea of jamming, he made an interesting point.

Dad: "Musicians just call out the key, and you just get up there and play. You don't even know what the song is. You just play whatever you feel. Improvise. Don't read too far into it. They call out the key, and then we jam."

Me: "What happens if you mess up?"

Dad: "Nothing. You just keep jamming. You go with it. Because if you don't go with it, you'll lose it, and the chords will just pass you right by."

I realized that we don't have to know how to play an instrument in order to apply the concept of "jamming" to our own lives.

Moving from New York to Charlotte was one of the biggest decisions of my life, and it was something I wrestled with for a long time before leaving. I could have come up with forty different reasons why I shouldn't have done it. But then I figured out that I had nothing to lose. I could always come back if I didn't like it, or if I failed, or if it didn't work out. It would have still been a lesson and a learning experience. I had no idea what I'd do in Charlotte, where I would live, or who I would meet.

I realized that, in the grand scheme of things, it's not even that big a deal. People pick up and leave all the time, moving to different countries and remote parts of the world. In the end, they experience amazing and often life-changing situations. They meet wonderful people. They expand their reach and grow internally in ways they never dreamed of. And guess what? Their families still love them just the same when they come home for the holidays. Sometimes those bonds even strengthen, since the time you do have becomes more meaningful. Relocating a few states away was really a small move. But jumping in without knowing all the answers or having everything figured out was one of the best things I could have ever done.

Leap and the net will appear

It's so easy to stay put and not make a move in life (literally or figuratively) because you are scared or uncertain. You can always find at least ten reasons as to why you should not do something. No one is ever certain. But those who go with their gut and take risks tend to be the most successful people. In life there will never be a definite answer on a tough decision. There will never be a solid "right time" to have kids. Your finances will never be "in order" enough for you to start that one thing you've been putting off. You'll always have "too much to do" to excuse you from taking that trip or enrolling in that class or calling that special someone you lost touch with. So forget about having all of the little details in place – because you never will. Just find your "key" and start jamming. Sure you may mess up or stumble a bit, but so what? As long as you're in the right vicinity, you'll quickly get back on track. If my dad refused to get out there until he knew all of the songs, he'd be in his basement practicing so much that he'd probably never make it on stage.

The keys always change

It's important to acknowledge that the keys always change. Four years ago for me, the key was moving to Charlotte. A short time later, another key was writing. I was never really sure where it would go, but I just found the key and started jamming. Now, there are other keys that are on the map, waiting for me to use my gut to find them and start playing. Every time, it's tough and scary. But it's always worth it.

The trick to jamming in life and going with your gut is to quiet down all of that other chatter in your head and pay attention. Allow yourself to feel what is going on without worrying about what you didn't do today, or what you have to do tomorrow, or what someone else may think. Not living up to your full potential and failing to follow through on things for yourself doesn't help anyone around you. Ironically instead, regret, resentment, guilt, and anxiety creep in, and none of those things are healthy for you or anyone else in your life. Many people are afraid that doing what is right for them would make them selfish, when ironically, the opposite occurs. It allows you to be happy and healthy, so you can now be the best version of YOU to all of those around you. Change is hard, and as with any transition, there will be some waves and rough waters. Expect this. Just hang on and ride it out until you reach smooth sailing. Remember, if change were easy, everyone would do it.

While watching my dad that night, I looked around and realized that there were many more people in the audience than there are on stage. (Of course, this is always the case at any concert you attend.) Part of this is obviously due to sheer talent that comes out of life gifts, and much practice and dedication from the musicians. But another part is because many people are too scared to get up there in the first place. So, what are you waiting for? Call out your key, and just start jamming.

My mother-in-law and father-in-law are celebrating forty years of marriage, and they couldn't agree more with the idea of having your own lives. My mother-in-law says it best: "You have to have your life together, and your life apart. This is a BIG part of marriage. Allowing the other person to do their own thing is so important. You can't hold them that tight. You both came into the relationship with your own separate lives. You can't ever lose that."

No matter how much you love someone, no one wants to feel suffocated. No matter how you slice it, neediness is not attractive and can often lead to resentment. Be careful that when your husband tells you he is going out with friends, you don't make him feel guilty. Husbands and wives will often say "yes" and play it cool, but then act in a way that makes the other feel accountable. It's just as bad as saying no. Instead, let him do his thing and use the time away to find an activity that you can call *your* own. This is a win-win: you won't drive yourself nuts focusing on what he's doing, and by partaking in a new activity that is all your own, you'll instantly appear sexier to him at the same time.

"Relationships of all kinds are like holding sand in your hand,

Hold it loosely with an open hand, the sand remains where it is,

The tighter you grasp it, the faster it trickles through your fingers."
~Author Unknown

Table #14:
Bling Bling Miss Thing
(A Few Words on
Diamonds)

"Diamonds are nothing more than chunks of coal that stuck to their jobs." ~Malcolm Forbes

The high price tag of a diamond is justified because we are led to believe that diamonds are a rarity. Each one is beautiful because they are insanely unique. So are fucking snowflakes. And if everyone wants one, designs one, and gets one, I had to ask myself: How rare could they possibly be?

When Greg asked me to marry him, I was twenty-four years old. I knew I loved him more than anything, and had a feeling that we would be married one day, but I just figured it would be a few years down the road. I hadn't given the idea of an engagement ring much thought, so I didn't know a damn thing about them. (For all I knew, "The Five Cs" could have stood for "costly circle of carbon-copied coal.") But he proposed to me with a diamond ring and I happily said yes. I thought it was beautiful, and I really loved that he chose it himself and helped to design it. But when the news started to travel and we began running into people, they all did the same thing: They'd reach for my hand, gush that it was "gorgeous!" and then toss my hand to the side.

I understand the impulse to see the ring, but I was really uncomfortable with this being the first thing people asked about. The whole ritual felt weird to me, and incredibly fake. What were they going to do if they didn't like it, anyway? Tell me it was hideous? The awkward feeling was solidified when I realized how often rings were talked about, and how they were compared to everyone else's.

"So-and-so has a HUGE rock!"

"I don't like so-and-so's ring."

"Wow, he must make a shitload of money to buy her that kind of a ring!"

"So-and-so copied my ring!"

Ick. It got to the point where, when people would ask to see my ring, I had to fight the impulse to turn it around. It's not that I didn't love it – it is a beautiful ring. And of course, not everyone was judging. In our society, asking and gushing seems like the polite thing to do, so some women may think it rude to *not* ask. And some people are genuinely happy for you. I wanted those who I loved and trusted to see it, because they cared about me. But I felt like I almost needed to protect it from all the judgment and comparisons.

The ring was supposed to be a symbol of love and sentiment. So why did the whole thing feel so awkward and tacky to me? Remembering how I felt, I hesitate to ask newly-engaged women if I can see their rings unless they are close friends. (I also noticed that this pisses certain women off, as their hands are already in their holsters, positioned to be whipped out on command of the draw.) But I don't ask because I don't want to be rude. I congratulate them on their plans to be married – because that is what it is really about, anyway.

Don't get me wrong, a genuine compliment is sincere and great – like when you see a woman stop another woman she doesn't know and tell her how she truly admires her ring, or when a close friend or family member wants to see it and talk to you about it. But the ones who just want something to gossip about? Steer clear of them.

What's a Diamond Worth?

"I have nothing against diamonds, or rubies or emeralds or sapphires. I do object when their acquisition is complicit in the debasement of children or the destruction of a country...It seems that almost every time a valuable natural resource is discovered in the world-whether it be diamonds, rubber, gold, oil, whatever-often what results is a tragedy for the country in which they are found. Making matters worse, the resulting riches from these resources rarely benefit the people of the country from which they come." ~Edward Zwick

You may have heard before that the diamond industry is engulfed by corruption and lies. But maybe you have not. I didn't, and when I finally came across some information and dug a bit deeper, I found facts that hit me on such a level in my core that I would be remiss to not share it with you, especially during this time in your life.

It looks so innocent

It's hard to imagine that an engagement ring – a delicate and shiny object, which is supposed to symbolize beauty and love and everything pure – can actually come from a place of exploitation and negativity. If you are familiar with the term "blood diamond," or the Blockbuster film sharing the same title starring Leonardo DiCaprio, you know what I am referring to. But if you are not, here is a brief explanation, taken from the website Ringenvy.com:

"The term 'blood diamond' refers to diamonds that come from war zones in Africa, and sold (typically illegally) in order to fund insurgent war efforts against legitimate and internationally recognized governments. These rebel factions trade diamonds with illicit arms dealers to fund their military action in opposition to those governments. Millions of deaths are linked to the rebel wars and trafficking of these gems.

"Labor exploitation has also been linked to blood diamonds. The scenes from Leonardo DiCaprio's Blood Diamond the movie isn't too far from the truth where African miners are exposed to atrocious living conditions and even worse working conditions. They don't have shoes, gloves, hard hats or flashlights, and their tools - picks, ropes – are simple and do nothing to relieve the back-breaking work. Mine shafts are unsecured and very dangerous. Accidents are frequent and many miners have been buried alive in these pits. At the end of a full workday, miners get paid less than a dollar. Finding a diamond may only get them $50."

Just this small bit of information could make one consider a bit more deeply the deadly effects of an expensive tradition, and may be enough to make a couple think twice about contributing to a terrible human issue. There is a ton of further facts and information about "blood diamonds" available on the internet, and if you are thinking of sporting a diamond, it might be a good idea to learn more about the process to decide if it is something you still find important.

But, aside from the "blood diamond" topic, I also wondered: how did the tradition of a diamond ring come about? How is it that this expensive object became such a staple in our culture – something that we've adopted on such a level that it is almost without question that an engaged woman gets a diamond ring? What I found, is that it was indeed no accident.

Of course, a tradition of this magnitude does not happen by chance, or good luck on the part of the diamond industries. There was a very strategic and carefully constructed agenda, and I can assure you, there is nothing romantic or sparkly about it. With any group trying to convince the masses of anything, there needs to be a meticulously structured plan formulated and carried out by a group of focused individuals such as advertisers and marketers. And getting the public to purchase diamonds as a symbol of love was no exception.

Hats off to those marketers and advertisers who put this plan in motion, for they were able to permeate our culture in such a way that their product has reserved its place as a staple in the biggest and most important events of our lives. Getting engaged? Get a diamond. Have your ten-year anniversary coming up? Get a bigger one. It is amazing how it is ingrained in our culture that we need a diamond in order to transition to marriage, or any part of our love lives, for that matter.

Edward Jay Epstein, an American investigative journalist, wrote a compelling essay titled, "Have You Ever Tried to Sell a Diamond?" The article ran in February 1982 (coincidentally, the month and year I was born,) in the *Atlantic Monthly*. In it, Epstein explores the ins and outs of the diamond industry, and how De Beers, the pioneer diamond company, accomplished selling the public on the idea of a diamond engagement ring:

> "In its 1947 strategy plan, the advertising agency [N.W. Ayer] strongly emphasized a psychological approach. 'We are dealing with a problem in mass psychology. We seek to ... strengthen the tradition of the diamond engagement ring – to make it a psychological necessity capable of competing successfully at the retail level with utility goods and services....' It defined as its target audience 'some 70 million people 15 years and over whose opinion we hope to influence in support of our objectives.' N. W. Ayer outlined a subtle program that included arranging for lecturers to visit high schools across the country. 'All of these lectures revolve around the diamond engagement ring, and are reaching thousands of girls in their assemblies, classes and informal meetings in our leading educational institutions,' the agency explained in a memorandum

to De Beers. The agency had organized, in 1946, a weekly service called 'Hollywood Personalities,' which provided 125 leading newspapers with descriptions of the diamonds worn by movie stars. And it continued its efforts to encourage news coverage of celebrities displaying diamond rings as symbols of romantic involvement.

In 1947, the agency commissioned a series of portraits of 'engaged socialites.' The idea was to create prestigious 'role models' for the poorer middle-class wage-earners. The advertising agency explained, in its 1948 strategy paper, 'We spread the word of diamonds worn by stars of screen and stage, by wives and daughters of political leaders, by any woman who can make the grocer's wife and the mechanic's sweetheart say 'I wish I had what she has.''

Just that last line alone makes me feel icky. Also, is not coveting a diamond really a "problem in mass psychology"? As I sit here and type, I glance at the ring my husband purchased for me, which quietly rests on my finger. It's pretty, and it sparkles. But knowing what I know now, would I feel I needed one in order to get married? It actually makes me ashamed that I did not know any of this sooner.

Greg and I openly talk about this concept all the time. From one angle, a ring serves as a widely recognized symbol that we are spoken for (and also acts as an excellent deterrent from Pervy Peter at the bar). But in essence, it can be *any* kind of ring that could send the same message when worn on our ring finger. Why a diamond? A diamond, as an object, is completely irrelevant to the fact that we are committed to one another, and does not directly impact our happiness or well-being. And honestly, the logic behind dropping the biggest chunk of cash you've probably ever spent on one item at a point where you are getting ready to plan for the rest of your life doesn't exactly sound like the best decision.

But for us, the point is moot. We half-jokingly say that we should sell the ring and donate the money to charity. But then we remember, he did put a lot of time and thought into choosing this particular ring for me. But even if we wanted to, how much could we get for it? Epstein explains:

> "Selling diamonds can also be an extraordinarily frustrating experience for private individuals. In 1978, for example, a wealthy woman in New York City decided to sell back a diamond ring she had bought from Tiffany two years earlier for $100,000 and use the proceeds toward a necklace of matched pearls that she fancied. She had read about the "diamond boom" in news magazines and hoped that she might make a profit on the diamond. Instead, the sales executive explained, with what she said seemed to be a touch of embarrassment, that Tiffany had "a strict policy against repurchasing diamonds." He assured her, however, that the diamond was extremely valuable, and suggested another Fifth Avenue jewelry store. The woman went from one leading jeweler to another, attempting to sell her diamond. One store offered to swap it for another jewel, and two other jewelers offered to accept the diamond "on consignment" and pay her a percentage of what they sold it for, but none of the half-dozen jewelers she visited offered her cash for her $100,000 diamond. She finally gave up and kept the diamond."

If I had known about this whole diamond business before being engaged, I think I would have done things much differently. Easier said than done, I know, and as with anything else in life, hindsight is 20/20. But two years after our engagement, and after learning this information, we purchased our wedding bands, and designed them without a single diamond in either one.

On a lighter note, perhaps the best part about my husband's ring, for him at least, is that he recently discovered that it doubles as a bottle opener. A friend pointed this out to him, and he had to try it. The look on his face when he used it to crack open that first Heineken was priceless. He now has a built-in beer opener, sitting right there on his finger. So ladies, if your man is not keen on sporting a ring and you are trying to convince him otherwise, let him in on that little nugget. It just may help you get to your goal.

What, No Ring?

"I do not want horses or diamonds - I am happy in possessing you." ~Clara Schumann

My husband's sister and her now-husband had been dating for about ten years when they decided that they would marry. Since he is Indian, and she Italian, they had a lot to consider when it came to the type of wedding, the location, and the details of the ceremony. They decided they would have a destination wedding in Jamaica, and would have two ceremonies, which they humorously referred to as the "white skin ceremony" and the "dark skin ceremony." It was going to be great.

Great it was. And all of it was possible with no engagement ring. Who would have thought that two adults could make a mature decision to spend the rest of their lives together, plan a wedding, celebrate, and be wed, all without a diamond?

When people heard the news that they were engaged, they began to ask to see her ring. She would explain that they chose not to purchase one. Some were shocked, and could not fully grasp the concept, as if the wedding gods would come down and halt her ceremony because she did not have one on her finger. Here is her personal experience:

"Not having an engagement ring wasn't so much of a decision NOT to have one, but I guess we just never made the decision TO have one. Actually I didn't really reflect on the reasons why I didn't want one before we shared with everyone that we were planning on getting married - it wasn't until afterwards that I was forced to think about it because of people asking. I really didn't expect this to be a problem. This may sound naïve but I just thought people would say stuff behind our backs, make glances or whatever but not outright ask me why I didn't want an engagement ring. The best was when a friend of a friend said to me, 'Oh, you're getting married!!! Let me see the ring!?'

'Oh, I don't have one.'

'OH MY GOD, I'm SO SORRY honey! Why didn't HE get you a ring?'

I was then forced to give this stranger an explanation.

My mom also tried hard to get me to at least wear my grandmother's diamond. 'It's not a blood diamond,' she would joke. I explained that the wars going on in Africa were not the reason why I didn't want a diamond, although it certainly didn't help her argument. (But while we're on the topic, it is this demand for diamonds that is fueling the wars in the first place. It doesn't matter where the diamond came from....if you're wearing a diamond, you are perpetuating the demand.) The main reason I didn't want a diamond is that I am really just not a jewelry person...I barely ever wore a ring in my life and a diamond has no personal meaning to me, simple as that." ~Kristen

My goal here really isn't to launch an attack against engagement rings. If it means something to you, then it can be very special, especially if it is a family member's stone or has some other sentimental value attached to it. For men, I can only imagine the rush that they get when they have that ring in their pocket, ready to pop the question. Everyone remembers how they got engaged. It's a happy and exciting experience for all involved.

I am not delusional enough to think that this little book is going to change the process of how we choose to become engaged as a culture, as a whole. But what I do hope is that it opens the door to encourage couples to break the mold and create new traditions. I was so excited when I read the below posting from one of my favorite food blogs, "Endless Simmer":

"Close readers of ES noticed that gansie went and dropped the f-bomb in her post yesterday. No, not the f-bomb she uses every day. The other one – fiancé. Eek!

Yes, it's true, our founding editor is engaged to the blogger formerly known as 80 proof! And since I think the ring looks like caviar, it's officially fit for inclusion as a topic on this food blog. For a more nuanced expert analysis, we turn to longtime ES commenter Mariah Carey:

'Bennett gave this ring to Stef with the explanation that it's not necessarily an "engagement ring." Rather, it's the ring he's giving her while asking her to spend the rest of her life with him. "Wear it all the time, don't wear it all the time, wear other rings as well..."'

So fucking cool. Congrats 80p and gansie!"

I think this is awesome, original, and personal to the couple. And, just for fun, below is a recipe and blog post by Gansie on Endless Simmer for a "Cosmopolitan Ring Pop," titled "Better Than a Diamond Ring":

"I'm not much of a proper lady, hailing from New Jersey and all. But in the South, there is etiquette all fucking over. For instance, brides not only get their

"ONE DAY" but they also receive a luncheon in their honor the Friday before the wedding.

This past weekend I attended a wedding in Durham, North Carolina and also attended the Bridal Luncheon. The woman who hosted the event owns a vintage shop, Dolly's, filled with eclectic housewares and get this, multi-colored tutus.

I'm not usually a sucker for cutesy, bridey crap, but this woman accomplished an adorably sassy feel by serving miniature bottles of Rionda Pink Prosecco with white and bright pink stripes; and for the bridesmaids, Cosmo Ring Pops.

Cosmopolitan Ring Pop

Recipe by Dolly's owner Jennifer Donner

- *2 and 1/2 cups cranberry juice*
- *5 T triple sec*
- *1 cup FRESH lime juice*
- *5 T cointreau*
- *1/4 cup favorite vodka*
- *1 and 1/2 cups crushed ice*

Combine all ingredients in a pitcher. Pour into ice pop trays, insert sticks and freeze for at least 12 hours. Remove from freezer and let stand for a minute or two at room temperature before removing from molds. This makes 24 – 2 oz ice cube tray pops, 6 – 8oz. pops, or 8 – 6oz pops.

No matter how you slice a diamond, it's still a diamond, and it has no direct correlation to the validity of your relationship, how much love you share, or how successful your marriage will be (if you would like examples to back up my point, please see: "Hollywood"). Instead, think about how important it really is to *you*.

If the idea of marrying without a diamond gets at least a few of us to think outside the jewelry box and do things our own way, then I deem it a success. And if you aren't sure how you feel, grab your partner's hand this winter and step outside as the snow is falling. Tilt your head back, enjoy the beauty in the sight of snowflakes coming toward you, and then open your mouth and taste one. Snowflakes are unique, they aren't available on demand (which makes them even more special,) they aren't controlled by a corporation. They haven't been extracted and cut and shaped and shipped and packaged and sold. And nonetheless, each one is perfect. They are sheer happiness – and they are free.

Table #15:
Hair, Makeup, and your Inner Fashionista

By now, you've probably collected several magazine pages and websites bookmarked with your favorite hair and makeup examples, which is perfect – you are right on track. Collecting ideas is the best way to go when it comes to fashion and makeup, and will give you a better sense of the direction you want to go when your big day comes.

When it comes to hair and makeup if you know you are particular and don't want to stress, go for a trial. Most artists expect this, and while some do charge, you may find others who provide free trials. As with every other vendor you will choose, do your homework on this one and confirm that the people you hire will be professional and reliable, and provide you with the best quality. Also have your dress picked out beforehand, so you can bring a picture to your stylist. You may have always pictured yourself with your hair down and flowing, but if your dress will have lots of detail in the back or at the neckline, you may find that an up-do would look best.

Be realistic when you find your favorite styles. Be honest with yourself in terms of not only what you know to be flattering to your face, but also the styles with which you feel most comfortable. And while of course you want to look your absolute best on your wedding day, make sure you look like yourself. Years later, in pictures, you will love your photos just as much, and the day of, your groom will still recognize you as the church doors open and you walk down the aisle.

One bride that I know, Amy, offers excellent advice: Ask your makeup artist to do your makeup trial in three stages. First, a natural look, then a medium and, if you still feel like you need more, graduate to heavy. Photograph yourself or have a friend photograph you at each stage, so you can see what you makes you happiest. It's commonly believed that you need to go heavier than usual in order to have your makeup "show up" in pictures, but some of the best makeup artists disagree. Instead, they suggest it is *how* the makeup is applied rather than *how much* makeup is applied, and Amy is a true testament to this theory. At her trial, she did all three stages, but on the day of her wedding she stopped at the first – and she couldn't have been happier with her pictures.

I had an interesting experience with my hair. The day of the wedding, I went with a completely different style than the trial. At the trial, my hair was done in a loose, low side pony that was very soft and romantic, but on the day of my wedding, my stylist recommended mostly down and flowing with one side pulled up. I was very happy with my hair and thought it turned out great. And I felt lucky it came out so nicely, considering my hair stylist showed up over an hour past our scheduled appointment.

Yep, this plays right into the advice earlier in the book about how some vendors are great – until the day of your wedding. The day of my trial, before I booked her, my stylist was all smiles and excitement. But on the chilly October morning of my wedding, my sister and I sat outside the empty, dark salon, peering in from the street for *over an hour,* wondering if she was planning on showing up. I was pretty cool and calm the entire day of my wedding, and can say with all honesty that it was this moment in particular that made me a bit nervous.

When she finally showed up, she pushed past us and unlocked the door without even saying hello. I let myself in, and as I set my pocketbook down on the couch she looked right at me and grumbled, "Ugh. These brides are killing me." Nice to see you too, sunshine! And what a great way to start the day. I'm sorry, but last time I checked, this was *her business.* She could have been a bit more accommodating, or at least apologized for being so late. (After all, the salon was about a half-hour from my home, where my makeup artist was waiting for me, and she was well aware of the schedule.) The hair stylist suggested the appointment time, not me, and even if she had a rough night and wasn't excited to be there, she could have at least pretended. Again, I was very happy with my hair, so I didn't waste time dwelling on it, but all in all it was a pretty crappy way to start off my day.

One bride, Claire, offers this useful advice for your wedding day:

"One thing I wish I had done was had someone take a digital photo of me on their camera or phone before I walked down the aisle. The hair and makeup people left unsightly bobby pins showing on my left side and also left some strands droop compared to the rest. Things that a.) weren't that obvious to the people that surrounded me but really showed up in pictures and b.) were at an angle I couldn't even see. This plagued me in some pictures and while I might have been a perfectionist when it came to finalizing our photos, if I had known or been able to see that one flaw, it could have easily been fixed. Even if you had a dry run, check yourself (at every angle you can) before pledging yourself to your professional photographer." ~Claire

Before you start taking your pictures, have a brutally honest friend or family member do a once-over to check you out and fix anything that may be out of place. Make any adjustments and, once you are satisfied, stop, walk away from the mirror and enjoy your day.

When it comes to makeup, a lot of women go for the option of air-brushing. This technique is great because it "sets" your makeup for you, so there really will be no need to re-apply or worry throughout your day. The downside to airbrushing is that you need to be careful if you are a crier. Always remember to pat, not wipe, your face if you turn on the waterworks.

I leave this table with professional advice from the best of the best. Her name is Rosemary, and she runs NY Prostyle Bridal in Dobbs Ferry, N.Y. She did my makeup, as well as that of several other women I know, and everyone has raved about her. She does hair as well (she did not do my hair, but after my experience, I wish I could go back in time and book her). Here is Rosemary's list of Bridal Beauty "Do's and Don'ts":

DO hire a professional hairstylist and makeup artist for your wedding day – it is an investment that will highly impact your pictures and video. Regardless of how talented your photographer/videographer is, if you aren't pleased with your appearance in the photos, then you will be dissatisfied. Your wedding is one of the most important events of your life, and you are likely to be photographed more on this day than any other. You should look and feel especially beautiful for the *entire day*.

DO ask the potential stylist to show you their credentials, as well as photos of their work and testimonials from past clients. You must be sure that you are dealing with a professional. Pros know the tricks of the trade, are experts in their field, and will deliver top quality services.

DO have service consultations, and schedule them for at least six months before the wedding. You and your stylist should choose your hair and makeup designs in advance - you don't want any surprises on the big day!

DO bring someone you feel comfortable with and whose opinion you trust to the consultations.

DO bring a picture of your gown and, if possible, a swatch of the fabric to the consultation. Your bridal hair and makeup should complement and balance your dress for a look that is consistent.

DO wear a top that is a similar color to your wedding gown to the makeup consultation.

DO pick a flattering hairstyle first, and then purchase a headpiece or hair ornaments that will work well with your hairstyle and gown. The stylist should have some sample headpieces to work with at the consult.

DO bring the headpiece and veil to the hair consult, if you already have them.

DON'T be afraid to share your personal preferences with the stylist during the consultation.

DON'T try to look extremely different on your wedding day. Your hair and makeup should only enhance you, not change you.

DO bring a camera and take photos of the work done at the consultations, so that you have them as a reference. (Understand that your camera and the amount of light provided by the flash will not be equal to the camera and lighting provided by the wedding photographer. Professional cameras show everything in their true colors.)

DO ask your stylist for a contract with your wedding date, specific timing, day-of location and balance when booking their services.

DO get a monthly facial to deep clean and exfoliate your skin.

DO have a good daily skin care regimen appropriate for your skin type.

DO drink at least eight glasses of water a day to help keep your skin clear.

DON'T stress out. Find ways to alleviate your pre-wedding concerns, such as doing yoga, going for walks, or meditating. Stress wreaks havoc on the skin as well as the mind.

DON'T get any chemical processes done in the ten days prior to your wedding - that goes for face, body and hair. You want to leave enough time to fix anything that might go wrong!

DON'T drastically change your hair color or style. Remember, you should look like yourself on your wedding day – only enhanced.

DO bring touch-up products such as lipstick, lip liner, lip gloss and oil blotting tissues to the wedding. That is all you will need if you have your makeup applied correctly. Everything else should last the entire event.

DO self-tan before the wedding if you want a healthy-looking glow. The safest method is to have your tan professionally applied (via a spray or a bottle) at a salon or spa. Remember to start at least ten days before the wedding - your tan can always be maintained if you like how it looks.

DON'T tan *too* much for the wedding. Being too dark in comparison to your natural coloring is not flattering.

DO bring a pain reliever just in case you get a headache from a tight hairstyle or your headpiece.

DO wear a perfume that works with your body chemistry. The fragrance is also part of your bridal beauty.

DON'T wash your hair the day of the wedding - wash it the day before. It is easier for a stylist to work with hair that is not "squeaky" clean. If you must wash it that day, then make sure you use extra hair product, such as a mousse or a gel, to give more texture to the hair. You should blow out your hair and make sure it is completely dry for the stylist unless he or she tells you otherwise.

DO wear a button-down or zippered shirt before you start your day-of beauty services, to avoid ruining your hair and makeup when it is time to get into your gown.

DO surround yourself with people that will help you stay calm during your wedding day beauty preparations – and this goes for your stylist as well as your family and friends.

DO relish being pampered and tended to. You are queen for the day. Enjoy!

Table #16: Honeymoon

After months (maybe years?) of wedding planning, the honeymoon is a much-needed vacation. It's a great time to kick back, relax, and get started on enjoying the whole point of it all – your marriage.

Maybe you've had your dream honeymoon planned for years, and that's all good and fine. But there are a few things to consider before you go vacation-happy and begin booking your reservations.

If your idea of a dream honeymoon is back-packing through Europe or island-hopping, this will require lots of planning and coordination and a ton of get-up-and-go. It may also require bouncing around from hotel to hotel along the way. You will most likely want to see and do many different things while you are there. If you and your future spouse love adventure and the get-up-and-go, this could be fun. But don't forget that no matter how great it all sounds now, you will be exhausted both physically and mentally from your wedding and may just want to kick back and relax. Are you sure you're up for the challenge? If so, then Godspeed, my friend – book away. If not, consider the option of taking an R&R honeymoon, and plan for a European vacay sometime next year when you can take your time to plan correctly and are ready to see it all.

On the flip side, maybe you dream of a two-week relaxing stay at an all-inclusive resort. But if you're a "doer," and all you'll be doing is lying on the beach, even Paradise can make some of us crazy.

Here are a few different options for honeymoons, and some advice from real brides and grooms on their experiences.

The Italian Honeymoon: Susan B

Honeymoon Destination: Italy (Rome, Florence, Venice)

Best part: Destination!

Worst part: We were in Florence on a Chianti tour on 9/11, when the attacks happened.

Recommend Doing: Exactly what you want. Go where you want to go – not where someone else thinks you should go (as long as you can afford it!). This is a once-in-a-lifetime trip. You need to enjoy it and look back on it knowing you did exactly what you wanted to do.

Rome was our favorite part! We spent a few extra days here at the beginning of the trip – it was worth it!

Venice was the best place to end the honeymoon. It was very relaxing, no cars – just walking along the canals and the gondola ride through the canals.

Recommend skipping: Florence was just OK. It is kind of the shopping destination, and we were not into that. We did very much enjoy the Chianti tour we took from Florence. Next time I would just take a day trip to Florence (train ride from Rome), instead of staying there for two to three days.

If you could do it over again, would you have gone somewhere else? Why? Would not have gone anywhere else! We would do the same thing all over again – just maybe tweak the details just a little.

The Greek Honeymoon: George

Honeymoon Destination: Greece (Athens, Santorini, Mikonos)

Best part: Hard to choose, but I guess I'd have to choose the scenery. Between the historic sites in Athens, the views in Santorini and the topless beach in Mikonos, there was always something to see.

Worst part: The Euro/Dollar conversion.

You recommend doing: You must go to Santorini. I can't imagine there is a more beautiful place on the planet.

You recommend skipping: The hydrofoil trip from Santorini to Mikonos.

If you could do it over again, would you have gone somewhere else? Why? Heck no… Greece was the right choice.

The Lazy Mexican Honeymoon: Dennis

My personal favorite, and the honeymoon my wife and I booked for ourselves. Eight days at an adults-only, all-inclusive resort on the outskirts of Cancun. Lazy outdoor canopy beds and amazing, on-site restaurants, here I come. Sexy, live mariachi music you could hear from your room at night as the curtains blow in the breeze, and drink of the day on the beach? Yes, please.

Destination: Moon Palace, Cancun

Best part: Being alone with my new wife at the pool, the hammock on our balcony, and fresh fruit with breakfast.

Worst part: Being on a bus trip back from the ruins with no bathroom.

You recommend: Leaving a full day between your wedding and leaving for your honeymoon, and then another day to do nothing before going back to work.

You recommend skipping: Isla Mujeras. Not even sure if it's been washed away by a hurricane or is in the same condition, but we were there for a full day trip, and were ready to leave in the afternoon, before the boat ride back, and before the bus ride after that.

If you could do it over again, would you have gone somewhere else? Why? No, though I would have made a commitment (date and dollar amount to be spent) on our flight home to go on another vacation together sometime, planned a couple of years out. It's tough to make it a priority otherwise, and would have been something to look forward to and save for together.

Mexican Honeymoon #2: Kelley

Honeymoon Destination: Cancun

Best part: The LeBlanc Spa Resort. It's an elegant, all-inclusive, adults-only, boutique style resort. It offers 24-hour butler service that will draw a bath for you and have it ready when you come in from a night out. The spa makes you feel as though you're in a world all of your own.

Worst part: Nothing bad to say about the hotel. We were disappointed in general with the nearby nightlife, reminiscent of a frat party.

You recommend doing: Swimming with the dolphins, organized through the hotel concierge. Shopping at La Isla Village, which offers upscale stores and scenic views of the canals.

You recommend skipping: Day trip to Isla Mujeres. Long waits for hour-long ferry ride to just be dumped onto a no-frills, dirty area of the island. When we saw the mechanical bull, we knew we couldn't stay there all day. My husband and I were so disappointed that we grabbed a cab to the other end of the island just to get a water taxi back to LeBlanc.

If you could do it over again, would you have gone somewhere else? Why? We would definitely do it all over again. The LeBlanc Resort in Cancun was the perfect destination for relaxation, pampering service, serene views and great food.

The Jamaican Honeymoon: Gina

Location: Negril

Best part: The beach, the resort and the people

Worst part: Bus ride there (long and scary – Jamaicans drive like nuts)

Recommend doing: Catamaran ride to Rick's café

Recommend Skipping: Nothing to skip – you can relax, you can scuba dive, you can snorkel, you can drink, you can play volleyball, you can play pool games or just veg. Whatever you want to do.

If you could do it over again, would you have gone somewhere else? Why? I would go back there again; we went to Jamaica for our tenth anniversary. Love the people there.

The Disney Honeymoon: Lisa

Length of stay: 13 days

Best part: The Segway Tour in Epcot, and just being with my new hubby.

Worst part: It was blistering cold…Florida had a cold snap, and only three of our days were bearable…I wore a pea coat, fleece, gloves and ear-muffs on most days, and was still cold!

You recommend doing: The Segway tour in Epcot, dinner at Victoria & Alberts in the Grand Floridian. It's expensive, but so worth it if you are a foodie. Also, the fireworks cruise.

You recommend skipping: The Christmas Sleigh ride at Fort Wilderness camp grounds.

If you could do it over again, would you have gone somewhere else? Why? Yes. I would have done a week in Disney, and a week somewhere tropical.

The Antigua Honeymoon: Chloe

Honeymoon Destination: Hermitage Bay

Best part: The most beautiful place I've ever seen. Wooden huts high in the mountains, with private plunge pools, overlooking a picturesque view of the ocean. The resort staff was extremely friendly and knew most couples by name. If you are looking for seclusion, this is the place to go....what seemed like a two-mile dirt road leads to the resort.

Worst part: 1) I got food poisoning after eating at the SAME restaurant for five days straight. There is only one place to eat. Not much variety. It may not have been the food and just a virus though because another couple we met there didn't get sick. 2) NOBODY TALKED! Out of the about 25 other couples there, only one couple was social. Everyone else just kept to themselves. 3) If you AREN'T looking for complete seclusion, this isn't the place to go. Once you are there, plan on just staying there. 4) It may not be like this all year, but the ocean water wasn't good for swimming. There was a red flag in the sand because the water was choppy and rocky. 5) Sleeping inside a huge bug net....if you're claustrophobic it might be a problem. 6) There was an air conditioning unit that kept the bedroom cool, but the bathroom was extremely hot and humid!!

You recommend: Laying on the beach, laying by the pool, laying in your hut (you'll do a lot of laying), and drinking the ENTIRE mini bar.

You recommend skipping: 1) Taking a hike on the "beautiful trail." After we walked the path, we came back with about fifty mosquito bites even despite wearing bug spray! 2) Trying to sleep without the bug net around your bed, you will get eaten alive!

If you could do it over again, would you have gone somewhere else? Why? Just to tell you, yes! But if you ask my husband, no! He wanted to go to Europe and I convinced him that we needed to relax and just lay around for a week, while he said we should go explore another country with tons of things to do. Wow, was he right! After four days, we were twiddling our fingers trying to find something to do.

The Cruise Ship Honeymoon: Melissa

Destination(s): Mexican Riviera: Mazatlan, Cabo San Lucas, Puerto Vallarta (Carnival Cruise Line)

Best part: Relaxing at the resort in Cabo San Lucas.

Worst part: Having to wait on line for four hours in the hot sun for embarkation and having to sit in a lounge for three hours to disembark! I have been on many cruises and this is the only cruise I have ever been on where embarkation and disembarkation were totally disorganized and chaotic.

Recommend Doing: Any excursion in Cabo San Lucas. The beaches are beautiful, the people are very nice, and the food is incredible!

Recommend skipping: THE CRUISE!

If you could do it over again, would you have gone somewhere else? Why? YES! I would have just gone to Cabo San Lucas and skipped the cruise! This is not to bash all cruises, I have been on many and love them, but after you get married, the only thing you want to do is relax and unwind. Having to deal with the embarkation process and being confined to a ship after all of the stress and chaos of a wedding was just not the best idea for us. Matter of fact, we took a second honeymoon the year after we got married to make up for our first honeymoon disaster! We went to Sandals in Antigua, which I HIGHLY recommend! The place is beautiful and the service was amazing!

The Hawaiian Honeymoon: Gina

Length of time: Five days in Kauai and five days in Maui.

Best part: Everything in Kauai!!! It's heaven on earth and nothing anyone says or any pictures you will ever see can do it justice. You just have to go! From zip-lining to touring the Na Pali Coast and Waimea Canyon to just hanging around the Grand Hyatt Kauai ….you cannot go wrong!

Worst part: The flights. It is a lot of flying. I'm not afraid of flying and can usually entertain myself pretty well with books, etc. But these flights were a bit tough at times. But…it was well worth it in the end and wouldn't stop me from going back.

You recommend doing: For flights, I recommend flying a direct flight and/or at least business class if you can afford it. Wish we had splurged for business class.

In Kauai: Spend as much (if not all) your time in Kauai. Do a helicopter tour, we didn't and I regret it. Rent a car, get a map and have some fun exploring the island. There is so much to see and so much of this island is untouched and just breathtaking. I highly recommend zip-lining, we used Outfitters Kauai and they were great! If you do a catamaran tour be sure to take Dramamine. I don't usually get seasick but I did on the catamaran and it can ruin the whole experience.

In Maui: Fun and beautiful but much more built up than Kauai. Go to Mama's Fish House for dinner. It is a great restaurant and the food and ambiance are fantastic. Be sure to make a reservation. Go to a luau. We thought it would probably be too touristy and cheesy but it was actually a lot of fun.

You recommend skipping: We weren't blown away by Maui, but some people love it so I won't say skip it all together. But I would skip the drive to Hana, it really isn't worth it. I would also not recommend the Hyatt Maui (whereas, the Grand Hyatt Kauai was the best of the best). It just isn't as nice as some of the other hotels, especially for a Hyatt.

If you could do it over again, would you have gone somewhere else? Why? Even though the flights are long…I would go again in a heartbeat. We have been back from Hawaii for almost two months and I still think about it every day. I can't wait to go back! There is something about it that just instantly relaxes you and you are constantly in awe of all the beauty around you. No site you will see is anything less than perfection. You won't be disappointed.

Hawaiian Honeymoon #2: Rula

Honeymoon Destination: Maui

Best part: (Do I have to pick one?) Road to Hana is my first pick. Everything was wonderful: the helicopter ride, the couples massage, stargazing with a telescope from the top of the hotel roof, snorkeling, attending a luau, submarine ride, shopping, and the beach...it was heaven.

Worst part: Leaving!

You recommend doing: Road to Hana on a guided tour and the helicopter ride (if you don't get motion sickness like my poor husband did.)

You recommend skipping: Hmmm...not sure about this one...what I regret NOT doing, however, is waking up at 3 am to see the sunrise from the volcano.

If you could do it over again, would you have gone somewhere else? Why? If I had it to do over again I would go exactly the same place and do the same things again, except this time I would add the 3 AM trip to the volcano to see the sunrise. That is one thing I regret missing.

The Hangout Honeymoon: Veronica

Length of time: One weekend.

My husband and I were far more spontaneous back then (going on eleven years). We didn't really plan ahead where we would go for our honeymoon. We had filled out registries at two locations, but many of our family and friends opted to gift us with money. We allotted ourselves $600 and drove down to Myrtle Beach, S.C. and spent the weekend just doing whatever we wanted together. It was more like a hangout honeymoon, which suited us just fine. We visited many of the local sites, and had a great time eating someplace different for each meal. We even went dancing. But no matter what we did it always started the same way, one of us looking at the other with a smile and asking, "So what next?" We always found something that interested us.

Best Part: Being together, spending time together with no real schedule, and talking to each other.

Worst Part: Only having the weekend to enjoy our hangout honeymoon.

You Recommend: Definitely doing what the two of you enjoy doing. Those exotic, elaborately planned honeymoons may be appealing, but we preferred the "no rush" approach. We drove at our own pace, enjoying the adventure along the way.

You Recommend Skipping: Elaborate honeymoon plans if they mean adhering to a schedule, unless that is how the both of you like it. Being together and relaxing is better than trying to run around to get to a ski lesson or be punctual for the captain's table. At least, that's how it was for us.

If you could do it over again, would you have gone somewhere else? Why? If we had it to do over again, I think more money and time would be nice, but I don't think we'd do that much differently. There were a few more places, like the botanical gardens, we'd have liked to visit at the time, but mostly it was the being together without any expectation to actually be anywhere that we liked best. The money we would have spent on a longer hotel stay, more restaurants, and admission to more attractions...

Checklist

Once you have chosen your destination, go through this checklist to make sure you've covered all of your bases:

o   Arrange to take time off from work. (Sayonara, bitches.)
o   Have your travel agent help book any transportation you will need.
o   Book your hotel reservations.
o   Update travel documents (passports, visas, etc.) if necessary.
o   Find out about trip insurance. (Even if you normally don't get insurance, make sure you get it for your honeymoon.)
o   Get any necessary immunizations for travel.
o   Book any activities/dining reservations you know are a must.
o   If necessary, change currency.
o   Confirm all reservations.
o   Arrange to have someone take care of your home (plants, pets, etc.).
o   Have stores you've registered at hold deliveries until you return.
o   Have someone get your mail, or have the post office hold it until you return.
o   Make sure you have all tickets and your itinerary.
o   Pack* (please see "Lists" section for a list of things you will need).

Money-Saving Advice and Other Tips

Look into the off-season. If you have the option of taking your honeymoon during the off-season, chances are you will score some big bucks in the savings department. We chose this path, and luckily our weather was great. If you are going to explore this option, try to stay toward the beginning of the off-season when the weather is at its best.

Ask about discounts. If you book your trip early enough, (usually six months to a year in advance,) certain destinations will offer a discount.

Watch out for holidays. If you are getting married on or around a holiday, consider waiting a week or two for your honeymoon so you don't get slammed with holiday travel rates.

Watch out for the water. Ah, serene beach days, the sound of waves lapping gently on the shore, your hair blowing in the wind – as you run for your life with your cheeks clenched to the nearest toilet. Don't let this be you.

Use a travel agent. They usually can help you book the best rates and offer any insight on cost-effective vacays.

Don't rely solely on your travel agent. Remember, while this person is here to help, they may also be receiving kickbacks from resorts they book. Do your homework. Make TripAdvisor your BFF, along with other wedding websites with info from real couples. There's nothing like real reviews from real couples to give you the scoop on resorts and other honeymoon hotspots.

Read the fine print. Susan can attest to this – she was on her honeymoon in Italy when the tragedies of 9/11 struck. *"If you buy trip insurance, read the fine print very carefully before you go. Who thinks of reading this, right? But, we were back in our hotel room in Florence after returning from our Chianti tour and realizing the extent of all that had happened back home, and we decided to pull out our trip insurance documentation – just so we knew what we were dealing with, since it became obvious very quickly that we may not get home when we planned (even though we were only halfway through our trip). Guess what it said? 'Void during acts of terrorism!!!' Even though it was a serious situation, it did give us a laugh!"*

Find out about room service. Many resorts boast that they provide room service, but what some won't tell you is that they may stop at 10pm. Consider the fact that you may be up late and be craving some late-night snacks. The last thing you'll want to hear from the concierge is that you're SOL. Do your homework.

Consider leaving for your honeymoon two days after the wedding. This will allow you to relax for a day with your family. It will also make you a bit less stressed during your wedding knowing that you don't need to make a mad dash for a flight the next morning.

Make your reservations in your maiden name. Even if you plan on taking your husband's last name, making your reservations in your name will alleviate any travel hiccups. You have the rest of your life to wait in line at the Social Security Office to have your name changed on all your travel documents, so for now, keep it simple.

Learn from "Friends," and "Pull a Monica." No, not the time she lost her blue nail in her mother's dinner party buffet. Think the time she and Chandler went on their honeymoon. She quickly learned the benefit in telling everyone they were honeymooners. Life is not TV, of course, but there are generous people out there working for airlines, hotels and restaurants who would be happy to provide upgrades for newlyweds. It can't hurt to ask.

Here is a great resource for planning your honeymoon: www.unforgettablehoneymoons.com

Whatever you decide for your honeymoon, I highly suggest taking one as a priority. It may be tempting to forego a honeymoon because of financial situations, but do all you can to make it work so you don't have any regrets. Nicole put her honeymoon off, and we can learn from her experience:

*"NEVER NEVER put the Honeymoon off for a later time. Budget this as a **necessity** no matter what your situation!*

"We postponed ours and a year later started a family thinking we would still go on our honeymoon (still haven't five years later.) Drop the kid off with the parents and jet. HOWEVER, it is the feeling that changes. Don't get me wrong, I will take an island getaway and have a hell of time at the drop of a dime, BUT it will never be the same feeling as a honeymoon just after the big day, without the responsibilities of a child and missing/thinking about my child the entire time!

"Reasons we waited:

-We had sort of a destination wedding to Miami with family traveling from all over the country/world and were too busy entertaining them.

-Extra cost (we didn't ask for wedding gifts and helped with some of the family travel, also paid for our own wedding)

-We thought an extra day or two in Miami would suffice, but we had a property there at the time and it was a second home we visited often (with home ownership responsibilities) so, needless to say, not much of a get away!

Wherever you choose to go on your honeymoon, think it through, take lots of pictures, and truly relax. If you are going to splurge in a certain area of your planning, let this be it. You've worked hard for it. As we've seen, while logically it may seem that the *wedding* is for you and your husband, in reality, it is the *honeymoon*. As Nicole mentions above, you will never get this time back!

When it was time to book our honeymoon, Greg and I looked into several options, but in the end, we wanted to just relax and get some sun. We ended up using a travel agent and booking a trip to Mexico. We stayed at the Excellence Playa Mujeres, an all-inclusive, adults-only resort in Cancun. This place exceeded all of our expectations, so much that for our four year anniversary that just passed, we went back again. It was fantastic.

Because we got married in late October, it was considered "off-season" at the resort and we were able to score an amazing deal. The week we were there, the resort was booked at only fifty-percent capacity, which meant it was even more peaceful. I was nervous about booking an all-inclusive resort because I have heard that the food usually is not of the best quality, but we were pleasantly surprised when every meal – literally, *every* meal – was top-notch. The resort was incredible, and was the perfect atmosphere in which to relax. We had options to do activities and excursions, but were in an environment that was so peaceful that we didn't feel the least bit guilty about sitting there and doing nothing for the entire day. We wound up doing a little bit of both.

I would recommend this resort and honeymoon one hundred times over. In fact, my cousin recently got married, and when we told them about this resort they booked their honeymoon there as well, and were so happy they did. We also recommended it to our best friends who just went this past July for their honeymoon, with rave reviews. Here, I'll answer my own questions below:

The Mexican Honeymoon: Our Personal Experience

Length of time: Eight days.

Best Part: The resort. It was absolutely beautiful, the people were wonderful, and the room was amazing. You will get so much for your money in this resort. We had 24-hour room service and an indoor/outdoor Jacuzzi, not to mention a bed on our balcony where we would take a "siesta" every day. One of my favorite memories is being in the Jacuzzi at night, and opening the wall of windows: there was a gentle breeze, and we could hear the ocean and the sounds of the mariachi band in the distance. Pure heaven.

Worst Part: If I had to list one thing, ironically, I'd say the spa. I preface this by noting the place was hardcore. The people who worked there were wonderful, the spa was absolutely gorgeous and extremely clean. But we signed up for a couples massage, and beforehand they put us through a series of "activities" to prepare us. It consisted of an obstacle course that was more like a type of "Warrior Dash." We were first put through a series of "pressure jets," then had to continuously enter and exit hot and cold water "submerging" pools. My husband looked over at me as one of the "pressure jets" was pounding against my neck, and he couldn't help but laugh as I tried to muster a half-smile and give him the thumbs-up. The obstacle course ended with a series of showers, one of which required pulling on a rope attached to a bucket that would spill cold water on our heads. I wish I were making this up. The eventual massage, however, was wonderful (and at that point, much needed).

Recommend: Taking advantage of the room service a few times. Not only do they bring you your food, but they enter your room and ask you where you would like it set up. ("On the balcony, Mr. and Mrs. Macaluso?

Or perhaps near the Jacuzzi?" "Um, yes please.") I also recommend para-sailing; the view of the resort and the clear blue water from up there is amazing.

Recommend Skipping: I can't say there's anything I did here that I wouldn't want to do again. Some did not like Isla Mujeres. It's not an abso-lute must, but we had a great time. Once there we rented a golf cart and drove it to the Mayan ruins, and grabbed a beer as we walked through the caves and explored. Afterwards we went to a local bar and sat on a "swing" that doubled as a bar stool and had a few laughs with locals. I also found two of my favorite beach cover-ups, and a decorative sexy statue of a man and woman – one of my favorite objects in our home.

If you could do it over again, would you have gone somewhere else? Why? No, we would have definitely done the same thing. It was just the relaxing trip we needed to recharge, and the perfect way to kick off our marriage. We had never gone away to a place like this before, so it was an amazing time to experience together.

Table #17:
Your "To Do" Lists

You're going to see a lot of "Bridal Checklists" out there, many filled with useless crap that will stress you out. During the time I was planning my own wedding, I noticed that everywhere I went, someone handed me a list. Time to register? Follow this list. Want to get married here? Use this checklist to give us what we need. Planning your honeymoon? Here's a list of items you'll need. While scanning the library shelves in the "Wedding" section before getting married, I noticed a ton of lists, and then stumbled on the mother of all lists, titled (wait for it)… *The Bride's Book of Lists*. Yeah! Because that's exactly what I needed: not only another list, but a book chock full of the fucking things.

Don't get me wrong – I'm a big organizer myself, and I can understand the value of the list. I use them to keep myself on track professionally. Using lists can help you to complete important tasks, prevent things from slipping through the cracks, and give you a sense of accomplishment and progress from checking things off.

But you know when they say that one seemingly small decision can change a life? Well, I just know in my heart of hearts that if I had purchased that "Book of Lists" in the library on that fateful day, I would have gone bat-shit crazy trying to fulfill every duty on those lists, probably would have needed to be tasered and taken away to an institution in a straight-jacket and, upon my release, embarked on a future as a lonely spinster with forty-six cats. (And I'm fairly certain I would have been shit-out-of-luck on those deposits already laid out.)

Instead, I followed only a few lists that I absolutely needed, and trusted that everything else would fall into place. I was confident that the important things would get done.

Here are two lists of things I felt were the most important, starting with a general timeline below. The timeline may look like a lot at first, but really it's meant to be a loose guideline to use during your planning, and will naturally help you cover all bases as you progress. Not all of it will apply to you, but take from it what you need. Some items you will dismiss, and other items you will realize you need to expand on.

Your Wedding Countdown Calendar

12+ months before: Engagement Bliss Mode

You're still on cloud nine, enjoying your engagement and trying to keep from swerving off the road as you drive while admiring your new bling. It's all peaches and candy. Be sure to enjoy this time. There are a few things you may want to get a head start on. So take a deep breath, and here we go…

*Arrange a time for your families to meet to celebrate and discuss plans. (If they have never met before, subtract three pounds from the stress you will endure.)

*Envision the type of wedding you and your hubs want, and draw up a budget upon which you both agree. Keep it fair, and be reasonable.

*Consider hiring a wedding consultant. Let's explore some pros and cons in doing so:

Pros

-They can save you lots of time, especially if you are busy with work.

-If you are planning a destination wedding, they can be crucial in coordinating details.

-You may reap the rewards of possible discounts they receive from vendors.

-You will have a neutral referee for when your family members share differing opinions.

-He/she will offer an unbiased opinion.

-He/she can act as an experienced buffer between you and vendors.

Cons

-The ones that actually do a good job are often expensive.

-This person is essentially a stranger. Do you really want a person you don't know to be all up in your business on this very important day of your life?

-This person may wind up not being in sync with your mother, in-laws, or others close to you, and in turn may create an additional relationship dynamic for you to worry about.

-You may get forced into things you really did not want, but were told you needed.

So it's really a toss-up. For the record, I did not hire a planner. My sister, however, did. I was fine without, and had great vendors that worked well together. Our reception hall also had two maître de's and a bridal assistant devoted to us for our wedding day, so I didn't see the need.

My sister, on the other hand, loved her planner and they did right by her – they worked well with the vendors, they thought of things she didn't think about. The clutch moment of the day was when a fabric flower popped off of my sister's expensive wedding dress before the reception even began, and her attendants were right there with a needle and thread.

Whatever you decide, do your homework. There is some serious money to be made in the bridal industry and, sadly, many take advantage of unsuspecting brides. Do Google searches, go to forums and ask real brides whom they can recommend. And proceed with caution.

*Think about selecting a wedding date. Be flexible, so you won't be let down. Before you go designing save-the-dates, make sure that both your reception and your ceremony sites are available, as well as key guests that will be attending. It's not a bad idea to check with your bridal party, officiant, and any vendors you are planning to use too. It won't hurt to have a backup date in mind, just in case.

*Think about your guest list. This will help you for when you are ready to scout locations, as you can ask how many people they can accommodate. You don't want to invite 400 guests to a room that only comfortably holds 250, and you also don't want to book a room that holds 250 for a guest list of 85. Also, keep in mind that about fifteen percent of your list is not going to attend. Many engaged couples cannot wrap their heads around this ("we'll never get that many regrets!") until the RSVPs come back. At first there is surprise and possible disappointment ("I can't believe so-and-so isn't coming!"), but then they aren't so upset when they realize that they may exceed the limit of guests and as a result may have to pay more. In the end, it all works out.

*If this is a tradition in your family, have an engagement party.

8-10 Months Before:

*Visit/book ceremony and reception sites.

*If you are having a bridal party, now would be a good time to ask. (And please re-visit Table #3 and give it a good, hard read before you do anything.) Once your choice is made, start thinking about how bridesmaids and groomsmen will be paired off.

*Shop for your gown.

*Decide on what type of entertainment you want for your reception and book it. The good ones book up quick. Contact your favorites and ask to see them in action at an event or other showcase.

*Start collecting ideas for floral arrangements.

*Research wedding insurance policies to protect your deposits.

*Reserve a block of rooms at a nearby hotel for out-of-town guests.

*Reserve a room for you and your new hubby.

*Register for gifts.

*Look into rental companies if necessary (for chairs, tables, linens, etc.).

6-8 months before:

*Book ceremony musicians.

*Research and book a photographer.

*Research and book a videographer.

*Research and book a florist.

*Select and order bridesmaids' dresses.

*Start planning your honeymoon. My advice: Use a travel agent. You may always book your trips on your own, but for your honeymoon, an agent is key.

*Send out your save-the-dates.

4-6 months before:

*Attend pre-wedding counselling (religious or non-religious).

*Shop and order invitations and wedding rings.

*Renew or get passports if necessary.

*Research wedding cake, book a cake designer.

*Purchase/order/make favors.

*Start getting ideas/shopping for bridal attendant gifts.

3 months before:

*Order the wedding cake.

*Schedule rehearsal dinner.

*Purchase/order/make gifts for bridal party, parents, and anyone else necessary (if this is a tradition).

*Hire a calligrapher, if you want your invitations professionally addressed.

*Attend your shower. Yes, you have to go. I'll never forget when my sister walked into her shower and let out a muffled, "Oh, no."

*Rent men's formalwear.

*Hire wedding day transportation: limos, other cars, etc. Think outside the box here. A friend of mine got married during prom season, and all of the classy limos she wanted were booked by teenagers drinking cheap liquor and trying to cop a feel. As a result, she had to go with the only option: a trolley. This wound up being absolutely adorable, so unexpected – and free. But we're not all that lucky.

*Purchase your bridal shoes, hairpiece, and other accessories.

*Address invitations.

2 months before:

*Mail out invitations.

*Write your vows (if applicable.)

*Book your stylist and try out big day hairstyles.

*Book a makeup artist, do a trial run.

*If you are planning a post-wedding brunch, work out the details now.

1 month before:

*Apply for a marriage license.

*Have your final fitting.

*Call all bridesmaids and groomsmen, and make sure they all have dresses and tuxes ready to go.

*Make last-minute adjustments/confirmations with vendors.

*Order or make welcome bags for out-of-town guests.

2 weeks before:

*Review final RSVP list and call any guests who have not yet sent a response.

*Plan the reception seating chart. Print place and table cards, or finalize the list with a calligrapher you have hired to do so. Cute idea: Go for a scroll or other elegant list, rather than the traditional place cards.

*Deliver must-have shot lists to photographer and videographer, and determine when pictures should be taken. My advice: Get all of the formal shots out of the way early and leave the rest of the reception for candid photos.

*Deliver a final song list to deejay or bandleader. Include any particular song you do *not* want played. I know someone who previously had a sticky situation with an ex-girlfriend whose name was Eileen. Needless to say, the bride had to give a particular no-no song to the band.

*Get your final pre-wedding haircut and color.

1 week before:

*Give the reception site/caterer your final guest headcount. Include vendors whom you will be feeding as well. Ask how many extra plates the caterer will prepare.

*Supply the location manager with a list of vendor requests, such as a table for the deejay or designated workstation needed by the florist.

*Call all vendors and confirm times and arrangements.

*Give the ceremony and reception site managers a schedule of vendor delivery and setup times, plus contact numbers.

*Groom: Get your hair trimmed.

*Attend bachelor/ette parties.

*Freak the fuck out. Right about now is the time when something triggers it. You're allowed to have at least one big one, so own it. Grab a bottle of wine, one or two of your nearest and dearest, and get it all out now. Make it epic. Then shake it off and get your game-face on. For me, the trigger was a serious cold, and involved me covered in glue and shrink-wrap thanks to a naïve gusto that overtook me months prior when I decided I would DIY our wedding favors. I had a fever, my hair was a mess, and I was armed with a glue gun in one hand and a blow dryer in the other attempting to shrink wrap mini gift baskets. The freak out finally passed, and for the gazillionth time in my life, I owe a thank you to cabernet.

2-3 days before:

*Bride: If necessary, have your dress steamed or pressed.

*Groom: Go for your final fitting and pick up your tux.

*Groom: Ask your best man to make sure all groomsmen pick up their outfits.

*Hand over place cards, table cards, menus, disposable cameras, favors, and any other items for setting the tables to the caterer and/or reception site managers.

*Reconfirm final details with vendors.

*Call the limo/car rental company for pickup times and locations.

*Arrange for out-of-town guests without cars to be picked up from the airport or train station.

*Deliver welcome baskets to the hotel concierge.

*Determine gratuities, and place them in marked envelopes so they are ready to be distributed on your wedding day (by either your husband, one of your parents, or someone close to you whom you trust).

Day before:

*Provide all of your wedding professionals with an emergency phone number to call on the day of the wedding.

*Write checks and/or talk to the wedding hosts about any final balances to be paid at the reception.

*Feel extremely weirded-out by the fact that you don't have much else to do, thanks to all of your planning. Pat yourself on the back for all of your hard work.

Night before:

*Rehearse the ceremony. Meet with your wedding party and readers to iron out details.

*Bring your unity candle, aisle runner, or other ceremony accessories to the site.

*Give your marriage license to your officiant.

*Attend your rehearsal dinner. Bring gifts for the wedding party and parents.

*Hand over the wedding rings to the best man.

Day of:

*Assign a family member to be the point-of-contact for the photographer and videographer to give the "who's who" in the family.

* Try not to be alarmed when one of your groomsmen travels all the way from his home, over an hour away, wearing Adidas sneakers and saying he forgot his shoes.

*ENJOY, LIVE, and BASK in the day. It will be over before you know it, so live it up. You deserve it!

Post-wedding:

*Prearrange for someone to return any rentals.
*Write your thank you notes.
*Sleep.

List #2: Packing for your Honeymoon

*Packing checklist:

Clothing
- o Bras and underwear
- o Lingerie
- o Bathing suits
- o Beach cover-ups and/or wrap
- o Shirts
- o Shorts
- o Sweater(s)
- o Pants
- o Sneakers (for excursions and walking)
- o Dressy shoes
- o Skirts (for easy access)
- o Dresses
- o Socks
- o Stockings
- o Sandals/flip flops
- o Workout gear (in case you are feeling ambitious)

Accessories
- o Belts
- o Scarf
- o Jewelry
- o Barrettes/bobby pins/hair clips
- o Bags (dressy & beach bags)
- o Sunglasses
- o Hat

For him:
- o Shirts (dressy and casual)
- o Pants (dressy and casual)
- o Sweaters
- o Shorts
- o Bathing suits
- o Jackets
- o Sleepwear
- o Socks
- o Underwear

Toiletries/Personal Care
- o Toothbrush
- o Toothpaste
- o Mouthwash
- o Dental floss
- o Shampoo/conditioner
- o Hair products (gel, hairspray, mouse)
- o Skin cleanser
- o Aloe Vera, in case of sunburn (tip: keep it in the fridge)
- o Brushes
- o Sunscreen
- o Moisturizer
- o Lip balm
- o Makeup

o   Perfume/cologne
o   Cotton balls
o   Cotton swabs
o   Deodorant
o   Razors
o   Shaving cream
o   Feminine products (you poor thing)
o   Pain reliever
o   Allergy meds
o   Prescription meds
o   Contact lenses/solution/glasses
o   Band-Aids
o   Birth control

Any Equipment for activities:
o   Hiking gear
o   Boating gear
o   Golf equipment
o   Ski equipment

Electronics and misc
o   iPods/iPads
o   Video Camera (bow chick-a-bow-wow)
o   Camera (plus extra film/memory card)
o   Cell phones and chargers
o   Books/magazines/Kindle or other electronic reading device
o   Electrical adapter (if necessary)
o   Travel journal
o   Guidebooks
o   Snacks/bottled water

Travel Docs and Extra Info
- o   Plane tickets
- o   Passports
- o   Itinerary
- o   Visas (if necessary)
- o   Confirmation numbers (for everything)
- o   Driver's license
- o   Currency

And hey, if this doesn't seem like enough for you, then purchase that godforsaken "Book of Lists." But if those creepy men come at you with the straightjackets, don't say I didn't warn you.

Back to the Dais

"…And you're so independent, you just refuse to bend so I keep bending till I break…" ~Staind, "Right Here Waiting"

There are two sides of the spectrum while maintaining a relationship with someone, whether you are just dating or have been married for years. On one end, we shouldn't be so wrapped up in pleasing someone else that we compromise ourselves and lose sight of our needs. And on the other end, we should remember what we are bringing to the table as well. During my chat with therapist Laura Frohboese, she put this into perspective: "Ask yourself: what do *I* bring to the table? Would *I* want to date (or marry) me?"

Bending too much for someone will inevitably cause you to break. But pulling too hard for your own needs could mean you risk breaking another. Finding the balance can be tricky, and it does not come easily in most cases - and that's okay. As long as you both openly communicate and respect each other, and tune in to your personal needs as well as each other's, the balance will happen naturally.

"Learn from others, as you would learn from your own mistakes."

~Kazi Shams, Writer/Poet

The case of communication and balance repeated itself in several patients whom therapists have seen, but one in particular was truly heartbreaking. Therapist Laura Lawson dealt with one recently-divorced woman who sat in her office on several occasions, hysterical, because she now realized the mistakes she made in her marriage. "She literally sits in my office and cries, saying, 'I nagged! I really did! I was never happy, I was always complaining…I'd give anything to have another chance.' But he's on to somebody else now." Lawson says this is not a "women bashing" example; she has dealt with several men who found themselves in similar situations. Humans are humans, after all, and we all make mistakes. It's up to us to acknowledge them before a bad situation turns worse, and it's also up to those of us who may be on the other end to call our partner out. Which leads me to our next table…

Table #18: Communication

Of all the ingredients that make up a marriage, communication is the single most important of them all. If you can't communicate with your spouse, you are setting yourself up for deep trouble in the future.

And by communicate, I don't just mean in the bedroom. (I'm sure by this point that connection is apparent – let's face it, it's a big part of what got you here in the first place.) I mean verbal communication and non-verbal communication; being able to voice your concerns and needs in a respectful manner, and in turn, *listening* to your spouse and giving him or her the same respect.

No matter who you are, no matter what dynamics make up your relationship, you need to remind yourself to constantly move between communication and respect. You will battle. You will disagree. Your marriage will not be perfect. But your ability to communicate as well as share a mutual respect with your partner is your lifeline.

Why "Marriage Takes Work" is Over-rated

People who offer up the age-old advice that "marriage takes work" often mean well, and yes, there is some amount of truth in that statement. But what exactly does "work" mean? How much is acceptable? Are we talking a part-time weekend gig, or a full-time job with no benefits or bathroom breaks?

Sure, marriage takes some work, just as any great friendship or relationship with a family member does. But you'll know the difference between "toughing it out" and growing together versus being a part of an unhealthy situation. Going into a marriage gearing up for battle should throw up a red flag. There are billions of people on this floating blue and green marble in the middle of nowhere, and we only get one shot at this life. You should expect some trying times ahead in marriage, yes, but if the bad severely outweighs the good, don't do it. You'll both be thankful later on in your lives that neither of you wasted the other's time.

You deserve to spend your time with someone who both challenges you and respects you, who wants you just as much as they need you. But it takes maintenance. It's a constant understanding that yes, it's hard work, but it should be extremely fun and fulfilling, too.

Just ask Pamela Haag. In her book *Marriage Confidential,* she talks about the curse of the many "just okay" marriages in the world. These spouses are not at each other's throats all the time over everything from how to spend free time to finances. But they aren't blissfully happy and crawling all over their spouse half-naked while feeding each other oysters, either. As Pamela explains to *Glamour,* "It's more about how you live in a marriage than whom you choose. I think people in happy marriages live like they're on vacation all the time, in the sense that they're paying attention to each other and trying to have some fun. Marriage should be enjoyable rather than just hard work."

Nobody's marriage is perfect, and we've all got our problems. In a nutshell, we are all weirdos - every last one of us. When two people find each other and connect, and decide they want to spend the rest of their lives together, it is a beautiful thing. Some call it love, or destiny. Some call it two completely weird individuals who were lucky enough to have their weirdness sync up with one another. And once that weirdness is revealed, they are stuck together till death do them part to keep the secret of just how weird they really are. But in all seriousness, you need a deep understanding of your partner, which takes commitment, lots of connecting, and a great amount of TLC.

Coming from "A Place of Yes"

My sister sent me a gift in the mail from Amazon not too long ago. It was Bethenny Frankel's book, *A Place of Yes*. The note attached from my sister said that Bethenny reminded her of me, and she thinks I'd like the book.

Greeeeeat, I thought. I've heard of Bethenny through the media, but to this day I've never seen an episode of *Real Housewives*. I assumed Bethenny was another spoiled, rich and delusional housewife taking up airspace in TV land. But, because of the recommendation from my sis, I cracked open the book - and I was pleasantly surprised.

One of the things she talks about is "breaking the chain." This refers to patterns in our lives that we do not wish to follow. While we may be more prone to certain pitfalls than others due to our nature and nurture (past relationships, inner demons, parent relationships, etc.), it is very possible for us to prevent ourselves from falling into those patterns in our adult life. With the right state of mind, we can not only acknowledge and overcome these fears, but sculpt an even better life for ourselves. In essence, it means "breaking the chain," and coming from "a place of yes." Taking Bethenny's theory and applying it to marriage, "breaking chains" and coming from "a place of yes" is essential in making it work.

One of the many therapists I interviewed is Dr. Beth Brearley-Parker, PhD. What I liked most about Beth is that she is very open with sharing the details of her relationship and is not afraid to talk about the ugly in her own marriage.

At the time of our interview, she had been married for thirty-one years. She credits part of her successful relationship to the fact that she was in her thirties when she wed, so she already had her finances together and so did her husband.

But the major credit she gives to their success is that both she and her husband were 110-percent willing to work on their relationship, and determined not to give up. She will be the first to tell you that the initial five years of her marriage were horrible. Her husband had been married once before, so there were issues there to deal with, and they had issues between the two of them as well. She wasn't in any danger, but there were rough waters to navigate. But they agreed from the start that they were in it no matter what, and divorce was not an option.

We enjoy the freedom to make our own choices, and in certain circumstances, the option to leave may be what's best. But going into marriage with the honest commitment that you will do whatever it takes is very honorable.

My interview with Dr. Brearley-Parker got me thinking that maybe, in saying our vows to our husbands and wives, we should also say vows to ourselves. Because your relationship with yourself directly affects your marriage as a whole.

The beauty is that we don't need to follow our parents' patterns. But we do need to be 100-percent honest with ourselves, recognizing those patterns and faults. We should give ourselves a break, and a hug, because we are only human. Then do what it takes to "break the chain."

Observe

"Here's how to shake your nerves during an interview: forget that you are trying to get hired. You're fucking awesome. But do you want to work for them? Do they deserve you? Go into the interview with that mentality. Because really, you *are interviewing* them." ~Greg (my husband).

Dr. Parker says that during the initial part of a relationship, especially for us women, we tend to focus more on watching ourselves rather than observing the person we are with. "Does he or she like me? Am I putting my best foot forward? Letting them see my greatest qualities? Can they tell I'm nervous? Does my breath stink? Where is this going? Did I shave my legs? Is he looking at me like that because he's falling madly in love with me, or is my unibrow growing back?" (You get the idea.)

Take a step back and be confident enough in yourself to shift the focus onto the other person. See if you like what *they* have to offer, and communicate well with them. Ask yourself: Is this person reliable? Does he treat me well? Does he put me down in front of others? Does he genuinely care about me?

Learn From Me: The Dumbass

In my early twenties, I had a relationship that taught me the above lesson the hard way. Let's refer to the man as "Jason." Jason seemed like a great guy. He was sweet, charming, and a smooth talker. He was so smooth that he could talk himself out of almost anything, not only in my relationship with him, but also through life.

However, for the entire six months we dated, I had a feeling in the pit of my stomach that he was lying to me. It wasn't about a particular subject or instance, it was just an overall bad feeling that he was dishonest, and it never went away. (This was especially strange for me, because I always tended to be too trusting in relationships, never really suspicious of others.) But since I never actually caught him doing anything, and he seemed so into me when we were together, I always just assumed I must be imagining things. I knew that he had a past with drugs, but he was very convincing when he said he dropped all those habits long ago, and I never wanted to hold him to his past since we all make mistakes. We jumped in pretty quickly and were spending a lot of time together from the beginning. But the longer our relationship went on, the more that nagging feeling kept creeping up.

I remember one morning in particular. I had to go the gynecologist to have a procedure done. (Disclaimer: Get ready for some TMI.) There was an irregular mole, er…down there, and while the doctor was pretty confident it was safe and "normal," he needed to remove it and perform a biopsy just to be sure. I was freaking the hell out the week leading up to the procedure, and I discussed it openly with Jason. He was great, saying I'd be fine, I'd have the procedure done and I'd come right over to his place and we'd watch movies, order take-out sushi and relax for the entire day. I was worried about nothing, he assured me. The night before the surgery, I left his house around 7pm. I went home, WebMD'd until I made myself sick, convulsed with nerves for about two hours, and went to bed.

The next morning, bright and early, I showed up at the gyno. (I'll spare you all the agonizing details, but let's just say that a male doctor coming at your most private place with a needle full of local anesthetic does not exactly induce a cooperative spread eagle. Naturally, getting started took a while.) When all was said and done, the actual procedure took about 2.5 seconds, and I was out the door. Hard part #1 was over, and now all I had to do was wait for the lab results. Somewhat relieved, I hopped in my car and drove straight to Jason's.

He wasn't there. I called his cell; no answer. I waited. I called again. And again. Where the hell was he? His car was here. Maybe he was sleeping inside? I banged on the door. Still no answer. I remembered that he had told me very early on in our relationship that he would give me a key to his place, which I promptly refused. (Looking back, it's funny that he came out with that so quickly, as if he was desperate to prove some sort of innocence.) By this time, my paranoid and worry-obsessed brain was firing on all cylinders. Was he sick? Stuck somewhere? Was he hurt? This was way too odd. I just left him last night. I sped home from his apartment in a panic, and I proceeded to call him pretty much every half hour. It wasn't about checking up on him in a jealous kind of way, either – I was truly worried that something bad had happened to him.

It wasn't until hours later that I finally received a call back. He was in Florida. It was a last minute decision: his (extremely shady) friend got him a ticket the night before, right after I left his house, so he packed a bag and went along. He'd be there for a week.

Now, don't get me wrong; I'm a sucker for spontaneity. As a matter of fact, I think it's a pretty redeeming quality in a man. But you could imagine how the letters **W T F** were rapidly scrolling like a ticker through my brain at this time. No phone call? No checking in? No real explanation, just felt like going away for a week and not even mentioning this?

Okay, maybe that's no big deal, I told myself. Besides, we were only dating for a few months. I said fine, and I'd talk to him when he got back, I guess. But as I hung up the phone, something punched me hard in the gut: *He never even asked me how my procedure went.* Going away and being spontaneous I could probably forgive, but not being there for me when he knew how upset and nervous I was? Unforgivable. If the roles were reversed, I would be there for him (or anyone, for that matter). Spontaneity aside, what would cause such an important piece of information to completely exit his brain? What would cause him to not even care about my well-being when he knew how distraught I was? There was only one answer, and it was always the same answer with him. Let's just say he may have been in sunny Florida, but homeboy was definitely skiing.

I found out later that he had gone on a total bender with some friends that began when I left his house the night before, and in this state, made the decision to skip town. But even when I heard the rumors and knew in my gut that something was wrong, he was incredibly skilled in talking himself out of situations and smoothing things over. Toward the end we had several fights, but it wasn't until a slight mix-up occurred that I had solid proof to give him the boot.

And it was all thanks to his sorry ass. I mean that quite literally.

You see, when he was on his way home one night with all of his boys, he had his phone in his back pocket and one of his ass cheeks scrolled to my name and hit 'SEND.' (It pays to have a name that starts with the letter A.) Because it was four o'clock in the morning, I was busy...I dunno, sleeping? So the call went to my voicemail.

The next morning I awoke to a lovely snippet of his conversation in the car with his boys. And in that conversation he was being cocky, saying he had to hurry home and decide "which piece of ass" he wanted that night. Since there were no more missed calls on my phone after that, I guess I wasn't the lucky winner.

The next day I confronted him, and of course he denied it – even as I stood in front of him and played it back to him, loud and clear, on speakerphone. I ended it with him, and after I left his apartment, I wished I had remembered to bring my umbrella as I was promptly showered by a giant shit-storm of information from others regarding things that went on during the six months we dated. Things everyone was afraid to tell me: drugs, cheating and lying, to name a few. Funny what information people will offer up once you are already out of a situation, and what information they choose to keep to themselves when you need to hear it the most. But I guess it makes sense that people don't want to get involved, and I guess it makes even more sense that I probably wouldn't have wanted to hear it anyway at the time.

The funny thing was that, during the entire time we dated, Jason repeatedly said we should get married. He'd talk about it all the time. He was seven years older than me, and felt like it would be a great thing for both of us. I can honestly say I was never that delusional. But at first, it was hard to spot the lies and other qualities I knew would never be right for me. And I can't help but wonder if I were a few years older (say, in my late twenties to mid-thirties): would I have overlooked certain things because I was more at the "marrying" age? I am thankful that this was not the case.

In the end, he was a dumbass. And he literally had a dumb ass (or a smart one, depending on how you look at the story). And for not trusting my gut from the get-go, I was a dumbass, too. Moral of the story? Don't be a dumbass.

Trust Your Gut

I've driven round in circles for three hours
It was bound to happen that I'd end up at yours,
I temporarily forgot there's better days to come
I thought that I would give you just one more chance

Cause I want, tonight, what I've been waiting for
But I've found, tonight, what I've been warned about...

~Dido, "See You When You're Forty"

Communication isn't always straightforward. People won't always tell you "I feel X," or "I need X." But their actions and mannerisms are still communicating to us. We just need to be willing to listen.

My experience with Jason is my personal example of this. I sometimes look back and wonder why it took me so long to trust my gut, and not just with him, but in many life situations and relationships. The answer is because my insecurities got the best of me.

Insecurity can intensify if you feel like you are on a clock and need to find Mr. Right. Most of the therapists I consulted for this book agree that women who set a time limit on themselves or succumb to the pressure of getting married and having children before it's "too late" often regret the pressure they put on themselves and those things that they overlooked, because they came back to bite them later on in the relationship. Many were afraid they would not find better, or they worried about how they would be viewed in the eyes of others if they did not settle down sometime soon. For some individuals, in their "last chance" mentality, they blindly overlooked dangerous red flags such as substance abuse and other abusive tendencies.

This all may sound pretty textbook, but remember: No one has these qualities written on their foreheads. If they did, people probably wouldn't get into relationships with them in the first place, as many individuals tend to put only their best qualities in the spotlight in the beginning. It's not like on your professional resume you'd write: "Royally fucked up that important board meeting, and forgot to schedule the CEO's flight that day. But hey, I'm a great team player." Observe the other person's character and values, and pay attention to your gut. If it doesn't feel right, don't force it. Timing is everything.

Like Two Passing Ships in the Night

Recently we went to New York for the wedding of my first cousin. She married the man of her dreams, and if you spend just a little bit of time with them, you can see they are meant to be together. We were at the wedding because the bride is my cousin, yes, but the groom is also a friend of my husband's. The funny thing is that they both attended our wedding – separately. Before their first date, before any get-to-know-you talks, before they even spoke a word to each other, they were in the same room watching us feed each other wedding cake. My cousin was a bridesmaid in the wedding, he was a guest. Neither of them brought a date. They began dating less than a year later, thanks to a re-introduction by my sister and her husband, and have been inseparable ever since, but we couldn't help but notice the clip in our wedding video where they walk right past each other, both looking opposite directions, through the Viennese hour. The first time we saw it, it was like watching a movie: "Holy crap! Just turn around! How are they not even seeing each other?!" But alas, no sparks flew over chocolate fountains and cookie trays. No matter how many times we watch, there is still no hooking of arms while feeding each other sips of champagne; no flirty glances from across the room. How could this be?!

The first answer, of course, is because life is not the movies. Most of the time, relationships don't just blossom out of thin air in romantic settings. Relationships often begin sloppy. Unconventional. Unexpected. We know this, but it still doesn't stop us from expecting fireworks. But the second reason is that it simply was not the right time.

Who says you can't meet anyone in a bar?

My husband and I met in a bar. I should really say RE-met, since we actually knew who each other were for quite a while — he was a friend of my brother's for years, although we had not seen each other in a long time. I had just gotten off my waitressing shift at a sports restaurant, where I worked with my friend Sarah. Like we did every Friday night, we would head over to Black Bear (a local bar) and talk about the crazy customers we had, while spending our tips at the bar on beer and cranberry/Southern Comfort shots (my drinks of choice at twenty-one). Because we would get out of work so late, there was no time to change our clothes or pretty ourselves up, so we were always still in our work clothes. Like every Friday we would arrive around midnight, dodging our way through the forest of Glamazons in six-inch stilettos, trying to avoid getting poked in the eye by a spike of hair that some dude spent forty-five minutes perfecting a few hours earlier, until we finally reached the bar.

That particular night, Greg found me through the crowd and came to say hello. Maybe it was because I wasn't wearing heels, and my 5'7 husband was thrilled to find someone he could talk to without straining his neck. Or maybe it was the whiff of buffalo wing sauce that enticed him, probably coming from my hair. Whatever created the magic, he took a chance to talk to me. I did not leave that night thinking I met the man I'd marry. I did not leave dreaming about the next time I'd see him, or how. As he walked away through the thick of porcupine heads and leggy ladies, we did not keep looking back at each other to catch a second glance. But on the flip side, I did not leave judging him and picking apart everything I wasn't crazy about. Being that I smelled like a blue cheese burger, I was really in no position to judge. But still. The relationship evolved gradually, and as it happened, it was the right time and place for the both of us.

I think that sometimes we expect too much too fast, or are too closed-down, and have a hard time letting things happen naturally, and in turn, we sabotage ourselves a little bit. And this type of thing does not stop at romantic relationships — it holds true for friendships, business opportunities, and conversations with strangers that may change your life. It's only natural that there are points in our lives when we are receptive to things and times that we are not. But as long as we keep an open heart and a positive outlook, and let our guards down just a bit, we will be receptive enough to let a little light in. And the next time you watch a couple cut into a wedding cake, or read about a wildly successful business venture, remember: it all started from someone being open-minded, and taking a chance on someone-or some*thing*-else.

"Ring the bells that still can ring, forget your perfect offering, there is a crack in everything, that's how the light gets in." – Leonard Cohen

Speaking of cracks...

Being that you are in marriage-mode, don't be afraid to let your awkwardness come out around your Mr. Right. If you can't be yourself with your spouse, who *can* you be yourself in front of? Don't feel like you have to hold up this "perfect" persona all the time. NO ONE is perfect, and it is the little idiosyncrasies that make us who we are.

I once had a conversation with a girl who very timidly mentioned that she absolutely one hundred percent could not fart in front of her husband. And it wasn't in a funny way – this girl was terrified at even the thought of a little toot accidentally escaping from her behind, for fear that he would…what? Freak out? Divorce her? Lose respect for her because she had a momentary lapse in control of her flatulence for a hot second? Maybe homeboy should've thought about that before taking her out for a hot date at Casa Del Mexicana? Your man should think you are the sexiest thing on the planet, but he better realize that you are a *real* person, and real people, well, they fart. Let's not be so serious all the time. Are you really going to let the occasional air biscuit come between you and your man? Laugh it off, and keep on truckin'. Embrace the awkwardness and embarrassment when it happens. Mr. Right will still love you, quirks and all.

Awkward Married Moment:

My husband and I were eating dinner, nicey-nice, in our kitchen. He leaned in and softly said, "Oh, come closer - you have a piece of hair in your face." He gingerly brushed my cheek with his hand in an effort to sweep the hair away. Only, he missed the hair. He tried again; same thing. He then decided to grab the hair and pull it away from my face. "Owww!" I yelped, as I grabbed my face.

Suddenly, we realized that the hair was not coming from my hairline. It was sprouting from my cheekbone. We shared a look of dumbfounded, wide-eyed horror for an eternity of 3.5 seconds. Then we stared at our plates for a bit and ate in silence – before we cracked up hysterically.

Back to the Dais: Just Do It

Let's talk about sex.

Sex is of course a taboo subject, but no matter who you are, a major key here again is to communicate with your partner. It may be embarrassing or awkward to discuss things, but it truly is important to be aware from the beginning of your partner's wants and needs, and to voice your own as well.

Therapist Laura Frohboese weighs in: "There's a big difference between respecting someone else's feelings and protecting someone else's feelings... What amazes me is how many people can't speak up about sexual preferences. They've been married for five years, and will say, 'She doesn't really want to have sex anymore, and I don't know how to talk to her about it.' But this is your spouse. If you can't talk to your spouse about it, how do you expect to be happy?"

The longer we let things like this go, the more difficult approaching the topic can become. Dr. Frohboese continues: "It's not like someone at that point is going to find it easy to say, 'By the way, what we've been doing for the past ten years…is that working for you? Because it's not for me.' I think it really comes down to the fact that we want to be nice and not hurt people's feelings. But in being nice, we aren't being genuine. The reality is that you're going to have to give hard truths to people if you are going to be close with them. I've seen people who have serious anxiety and depression issues…they feel trapped. The thought of speaking up feels completely overwhelming."

Voicing your honest opinions to your spouse and coming clean with your wants and needs can lead to all sorts of anxiety initially, and this is normal. But the irony is that, in many cases, you will find that your significant other will be open and receptive – and may even want the same thing. They just haven't figured out the best way to say it to *you* yet.

Have you ever heard a song that you have known for years and years – but for some reason, one day it hits you on a totally different level? Call me crazy (and by now you know I am), but this happened to me one day at the pool when I heard on the radio a song by Rupert Holmes called "Escape." You may know it better as "The Pina Colada Song." Yup. That's the one.

Have you ever truly listened to the irony in the lyrics? As I lay there humming the tune, it dawned on me what the song was actually about. Play that tune in your head, and pay attention to the *story* in the lyrics below:

"Escape" (The Pina Colada Song,) by Rupert Holmes

I was tired of my lady
we'd been together too long
like a worn out recording of a favorite song
So while she lay there sleeping,
I read the paper in bed;
and in the personal columns,
there was this letter I read:

If you like Pina Coladas
and getting caught in the rain,
If you're not into yoga,
if you have half a brain,
If you like making love at midnight,
in the dunes of the Cape,
then I'm the love that you've looked for,
write to me and escape.

I didn't think about my lady,
I know that sounds kinda mean
but me and my old lady,
had fallen into that same old dull routine
So I wrote to the paper,
took out a personal ad,
and though I'm nobody's poet,
I thought it wasn't half bad:

Yes, I like Pina Coladas,
and getting caught in the rain,
I'm not much into health food,
I am into champagne.
I've got to meet you by tomorrow noon,
and cut through all this red tape,
at a bar called O'Malley's,
and we'll plan our escape.

So I waited with high hopes,
and she walked in the place
I knew her smile in an instant,
I knew the curve of her face
It was my own lovely lady,
and she said, "Aw, it's you!"
and we laughed for a moment,
and I said, "I never knew..."

That you liked Pina Coladas,
and getting caught in the rain,
and the feel of the ocean,
and the taste of champagne
If you like making love at midnight,
in the dunes of the Cape,
you're the lady I've looked for,
come with me and escape.

If you like Pina Coladas
and getting caught in the rain,
If you're not into yoga,
if you have half a brain
If you like making love at midnight,
in the dunes of the Cape,
then I'm the love that you've looked for,
write to me and escape.

You'll probably never listen to that song the same way again. And sure, it's (admittedly) a cheesy example. But I hope you'll think of it when you are having a hard time coming clean to your significant other about your wants and needs from your relationship. Remember, you are together for a reason. There may be periods that you become a bit disconnected, but you are more alike than you may think. As long as you are sensitive to your spouse's feelings and careful in your approach, your relationship can be taken to the next level – and you may be surprised that your spouse has felt the same way as you all along.

Dr. Frohboese suggests that we write a personal ad for ourselves. In it, answer the following questions: What are your wants and needs? What do YOU bring to the table? Have your husband do the same, then discuss your answers. Who knows? Maybe you'll find that you both like Pina Coladas.

Awkward and Unsolicited Sex Advice from My Mother

It was a beautiful day outside in Thornwood, N.Y. I was fifteen years old, hanging out at the house with my seventeen-year-old sister. It was on this fateful day that my mom decided it was time to talk to us about sex.

It's worth pointing out that my mother is not exactly open when it comes to this type of thing. I don't know if it was an instinctual denial of the fact that we were growing up and her desire to keep us little kids forever, but she tended to avoid these sorts of topics.

She sat my sister and I down, and I remember being really nervous. What the hell was she going to tell us? Were she and Dad getting a divorce? Did I do something bad? After pacing for a few moments, she gathered her thoughts, took a deep breath, and then, in her thick New York accent, out poured, "Your thighs…are your two best friends. They always…stick… together."

My sister and I sat there, dumbfounded, processing the sentence she just uttered. She followed this up with a death stare, as she dipped her brow, pointed her finger at us, and said "Alright? *Alright*? You got it?" That was as far as her sex talk went. My sister and I exchanged an awkward glance, mumbled something about having to go meet some friends, and off we went.

Table #19:
Useful Tips

There are things that people will tell you to think about ahead of time for your wedding, which is great. But there are a slew of things that no one really tells you. So, I've put together a list of tips from my own experience and the experience of others to help your day go as smoothly as possible. So, without further ado, some useful tips to remember while planning your wedding.

*"Get lots of sleep the week before your wedding, because the night before, you won't sleep a wink! You'll have such an adrenaline rush and the day-of will be one of the most exciting yet exhausting days of your life!" ~Chloe

*This is an EXCELLENT one, and I credit it to the amazing wedding photographer Ricky Restiano. It applies to any bride, no matter what type of wedding you have. Ready? Pee facing the opposite way. Think about it: It's hard enough to squat, never mind when you can't even find your own legs under a parachute of bridal gown material. Approaching the toilet head-on will make your tinkles a bajillion times easier. It's the little things!

*Do not, I repeat, DO NOT share information about your wedding with anyone other than those you hold closest to you. Almost every post-bride can relate to being burned when they innocently shared their ideas and excitement with a "friend" or family member who was also getting married – who then stole the idea right from under them. Don't think for a second that this does not happen, because it does – and it will. When it comes to weddings, people will never cease to surprise you. I could fill a whole book with the feedback I received from brides on this one, with my own experiences included, but let's hear Margaret's story:

"It's funny how weddings bring out the insecurities in some people. I had the unfortunate experience of having a sister-in-law who apparently doesn't have a creative thought of her own and felt that the key to planning a great wedding was to just use whatever ideas I had.

"I got engaged and was pretty much done planning my wedding when my brother got engaged to my now sister-in-law. They decided to plan their wedding before mine, which was fine with me, until their wedding started to look a little too familiar.

"It wasn't the little things that bothered me, like the fact that she registered for the same china that we did, or that she was going to plan their honeymoon at the same destination as us. I even let it slide when she had negative things to say about the bridesmaids dress that I chose, then chose basically the exact same style dress just different fabric for their wedding. None of this pushed me quite over the edge. Not until the catering hall fiasco, that is.

"I had already chosen my date and my venue. My sister-in-law made sure she voiced her opinions about the catering hall I had chosen: "The food is hit or miss," "It's overpriced for what you get," "The service isn't very good." So you can imagine my surprise when I received a phone call from my brother telling me that the catering hall they wanted wasn't available on the day they wanted, so they were going to book my catering hall instead. That was my breaking point! I in no uncertain terms told my brother he was crazy if he thought he was going to get married before me, at the same catering hall. The catering hall that his

fiancé did nothing but knock from day one! Needless to say, after my tirade my brother thought better of the idea and they decided to go with a completely different venue. So, my advice: Don't share your ideas if you don't want someone else to use them!" ~Margaret

* "This is your wedding day, even if someone else is paying for it. If something is important to you, but not the person paying for the wedding, pay for that item yourself." ~Susan

*The week before your wedding, have half a bowl of ice cream each night. No, I'm not trying to make you a fatty before your wedding. As crazy as this may sound, you will lose weight in the home stretch due to pre-wedding stress. And since your final fitting has probably come and gone, you want your dress to fit you when you walk down the aisle. I can't tell you how many brides I have seen who could fit their bouquet down the front of their dress if they tried because of unplanned weight loss in between their last fitting and their big day.

* "There will be drama when you blend two families and their different ways of celebrating. Decide what is important to you and your future spouse and work together. If there is a disagreement, just move on to the next thing, not giving in to pressure from either side. Easier said than done, but there are so many details to be involved in, just move on to the next thing – that person will get over it." ~Susan

* "Never lose sight of the big picture & don't sweat the small stuff! It's easy to stress yourself over the ever-so-important decision between passion fruit mousse and chocolate mousse for your cake. Guess what? You think anybody said to me 'WOW, I just LOVED the passion fruit mousse cake!'?" ~Maryann

*Eat, brush your teeth, and do everything else *before* you put on your dress to avoid any stains or mishaps. And if you are going to eat something once your dress is on, put a towel or something over you just in case. At my sister's wedding, they wrapped her in a tablecloth while she ate in the bridal suite, just to be safe.

* "Don't give up what you want because of what everyone makes you think a wedding should be. Don't sell out. Find a place that checks as many of your 'dream' boxes as you can. It's okay if the perfect place doesn't include every little thing you think your guests need to have a good time or need to see at your wedding or else they will judge you. It isn't about them. It's about you and your fiancé and what you guys want. Some of your guests will love everything about your wedding and there will always be others who will find something to complain about. I say come to terms with that and move on...find a place that makes you happy." ~Gina

* "Keep the birdcage (read: money holder) away from the entrance. You don't want anybody stealing your gifts (staff or anyone else). A lot of people will put cash in the envelopes, or make the checks out to cash." ~Steve

* "Keep it classy. One of the tackiest things I ever saw was a bride who spent much of her day bad-mouthing one girl in particular who was at the wedding. The trash-talking continued all the way through the day – in between limo rides, cake-cutting, and first dances, the venom spewed. I happened to be in the car with the bride and groom on their way to the hotel at the end of the night, and still, the shit-talking continued. I couldn't help but feel sorry for her husband. We all have people around us (hopefully not more than one) that will add drama to our day, but we need to know when to drop it for our own sake – not to mention, the sanity of those around us...Once we arrived at the hotel, this bride proceeded to jump the entire line, storm up to the check-in counter, and demand, 'I am the bride, I want my room NOW.' I don't care how pretty you look – classlessness doesn't wear well on anyone." ~Jasmine

Listen up, Ladies: A Very Valuable Q&A with the Amazing Ricky Restiano of Ricky Restiano Photography

Alessandra Macaluso: What would be the first piece of advice you would give to brides when it comes to photography?

Ricky Restiano: Meet the photographer and like him or her. Really if you don't like them at the meeting you're going to hate them for 12 hours on your wedding day.

AM: What would be the first piece of advice you would give to brides regarding the planning process in general?

RR: Have a real idea of your budget. When you start planning, everything seems feasible until the payments start coming in.

AM: Bridal party or no bridal party - what do you prefer as a vendor, and why?

RR: Normal-sized bridal parties are fine. No offense to anybody who had or is having one, but seriously when did the 30-person bridal party come back into style?

AM: What's the most valuable thing you taught a bride?

RR: How to be sexy in photographs.

AM: Any tips for couples, for when being photographed?

RR: Don't stress about the photos. As long as you picked a photographer you're into, the photos will be great. Also, don't second-guess your decision. If you picked a traditional photographer, go with it. You chose that style for a reason. If you picked an edgy photographer, trust that person to do what he/she does best.

Also, practice. If you are stressing about the photo part of the day you should really practice. Have a friend shoot you, or even book an engagement session. Don't always smile in photos. There is no photo rule that you have to have a big cheese. *(I wish someone would have told me this!!!)*

AM: Any advice to offer grooms?

RR: Have a drink before the ceremony.

AM: What's your favorite kind of wedding to shoot, and why?

RR: I like weddings when the photo shoot part of the day is planned out. We are not scrambling to get a few images in. The bride and groom make the photo shoot a big part of the day and we can really shine.

AM: In your opinion, aside from photographer/videographer, what is the next most important thing a couple should spend their money on?

RR: Entertainment!

Table #20:
The After Party

"So don't forget who's taking you home, and in whose arms you're gonna be;

So darling, save the last dance for me…" ~Michael Buble

Here we are, nearing the end of this book. I hope you have found it useful on your journey of wedding planning and bridal business. Now that the party's over, I hope you've had a great time.

My goal in writing this book was to show you wedding planning from as many angles as possible, and offer a real and raw look at weddings – one that magazines and bridal planners don't normally touch on. To encourage you to step out of the assembly line of brides, and to let your uniqueness shine. To give you tools for dealing with tricky situations. And to allow myself and other newlyweds to open up and offer honest experiences and advice about not only the wedding, but the marriage. If this book helps at least one bride stay true to herself, or helps a couple through a difficult time while adjusting to married life, then I deem it a success.

So, do you, bride-to-be or newlywed, take this book, as a sign of truth and guidance, to have and to hold? I hope so, because I do.

We would be rude hosts if we did not go around the room and say goodbye to our tables, so let's take a walk back around to revisit and sum up what we've covered.

Table #1: The calm before the storm. While wedding planning can be an exciting time in your life, our society has also made it one of the most stressful. Take your time to simply enjoy being engaged, because you will never have this opportunity again. You will be influenced by planners, vendors, family and friends, so set the bar with your spouse-to-be and always check back in with each other to make sure it's heading in a direction you are both comfortable with.

Table #2: Pre-Planning Checklist. Get prepared for what's to come, and talk with your fiancé about how you want to handle issues as they arise. There are many things here that, if considered at this point, will help you throughout your planning days.

Table #3: Bridal Party. Whether you decide to have two or twenty, do what works for you and don't fall flat on your face while trying to accommodate everyone. Maybe you have an easy-breezy crew that will be super helpful. But maybe your crew, as much as you love them, is full of drama queens and flake-outs. You don't want to be stressed about your bridal party on a day that is so intimate to you, so think things through before you commit. It's perfectly fine to simply have a best man and a maid of honor. When you do settle on a bridal party, treat them with respect and remember that they have lives as well. Hopefully you've gained some insight here by reading about the experiences of others.

Table #4: In-laws. Love them or hate them, you are marrying into the family and you have to deal with them. If you come from a positive place when you interact with them, your life will be much easier, and you will save yourself a ton of stress in your marriage. Remember, they are not and do not have to become your best friends. Do your best to make your time with them as painless as possible so you can all get on with your lives when the visit is over. And keep boundaries. No one should have a say in your marriage other than you and your husband. Use the tactics in this chapter to navigate through these sometimes murky waters.

Table #5: Haters. Yep, they exist, and have a tendency to flare up like a hemorrhoid when someone they know gets married. Maybe it's jealousy, maybe it's competition, or maybe they just like to cause trouble, but no matter the reason, their negative energy doesn't need to affect you on one of the most beautiful days of your life. Take from this chapter the tools you need to stay positive and keep the haters at bay.

Table #6: Ceremony. Since we all come from different walks of life, there are no set rules for your ceremony. No matter what you decide, make sure your ceremony honors both sides (if even just a little), reflects your personal beliefs and rituals, and means something to the two of you. It doesn't need to be elaborate or lengthy. And don't forget to write a thank-you card to your officiant.

Table #7: The Reception. Put your business hat on before booking a hall. Envision attending a wedding at the hall as a guest, to give you a better idea of how people will experience your wedding. Read the fine print to determine important things, such as deposit refund policies, to avoid a potential headache down the road.

Table #8: Bridal Gown Shopping. Keep the amount of people in your group down to a minimum, and search deep within yourself to find your own personal style. Stay grounded and do your best to find a dress that reflects you. Use the tips in this chapter to discover your style and to help you "say yes" to the dress.

Table #9: Vendors. In an endless sea of vendors competing for jobs in the bridal industry, choosing the right ones can be difficult. Do your homework and put in a bit of research before booking blindly. Go visit the band at a showcase. Spend time with your florist. Join online forums for real advice and reviews. Vendors can make or break your big day. Ask trusted friends and loved ones for recommendations. Read the real-life stories in this chapter for reference. Once you book, don't be afraid to check in with them every once in a while to go over details.

Table #10: Showers & Big-Box Marts. Being married marks a new beginning, so you will surely need a few things from a registry. It's understandable. Just use your discretion on what you really need and what will complicate your life. And don't be afraid to do things untraditionally. Use this chapter to help you think outside the box – the big box marts, that is.

Table #11: Etiquette, & the Etiquette-less. Hopefully here you learned some things you may not have known before you began this process. Sometimes you find you have offended someone and you didn't even know it. It's good to have a heads up on your bridal etiquette. After all, you are new at this! Also, when it comes to the etiquette of others, remember: brace yourself. You know by now that weddings conjure up some weird shit in people. Some will say and do the most ridiculous things, thinking they are helping you or that they aren't acting as though they swallowed paint thinner and a rum chaser. Take a deep breath, remember the antics so you can laugh about it later, then keep on truckin'. They really did just do that, and they really are nuts.

Table #12: Your Mental Health. It's so easy to take a swan-dive off into the deep end. Even the most cool and collected among us can turn loopy once we are boob-deep in wedding planning. So before you find yourself locked in a closet talking to old pillows about your plans to elope to Vegas, take notes on this chapter and remember to take care of yourself. It's an important day of your life and you want it to be wonderful and fantastic, but at the end of the day, it doesn't define you and isn't worth your sanity. It's just a wedding, and no matter what sort of shit goes down, your husband will still love you.

Table #13: Here Comes the Groom. The planning process takes a toll on not just you, but your partner as well. Good thing people are checking in on him too! Wait a minute, that's right – no one is actually checking in on him. Who really cares what the groom is going through during the chaos of planning a wedding? You do, and that's why it's a good idea to make sure he's cool with what's going on at all times. Sure, some guys don't really care or don't get involved, but it doesn't mean they aren't affected. Get him involved as much as he wants to be, and make sure he's comfortable with what's going on. Most guys won't ask for that, but it will mean the world to them if you show them that while everyone else is focusing on you, you are focusing on him.

Table #14: Bling Bling Miss Thing. There is so much to think about when it comes to rings and it's easy to get caught up in the hype. Before you make any choices, hopefully some of the info in this chapter will give you a glance from all angles and help you decide what is really important to you and your spouse. And read this chapter, because it could help you deal with haters who just want to scrutinize your ring and talk smack. Oh yes, they walk among us.

Table #15: Hair, Makeup & Your Inner Fashionista. So many choices! So much pressure! Take some hard core advice from recent brides, and some tips from the best in the industry, here.

Table #16: Your Honeymoon. So many choices! So much pressure! (Seeing a pattern yet?) But overall, this was one of my favorite chapters to write. I loved hearing everyone's stories of their personal honeymoons, recommendations, and planning. Do some research, ask the right questions, and then get ready to relax – you'll need it. And remember: no matter what, it's the two of you so you are going to have a blast.

Table #17: Your "To-Do" Lists. Ah, so many lists, so little time. Use this chapter to narrow down what *you* really need for *your* personal planning process; then tell everyone else to shove it and go enjoy a margarita. It's easy to get flustered and there are plenty of people whose jobs are to fluster you, but I have made it my job to prepare you and be sure you are forewarned.

Table #18: Communication No matter what your relationship is like, no matter who your partner is, no matter what you do, say, feel, or act, one thing is constant – communication is by far the most important element to your relationship, and always will be. Read through this chapter to learn from the trials of others and think about your own relationships. When I say relationships I don't think you are a polygamist – I pluralize because communication applies to all of your relationships. Family, friends, business partners…it doesn't matter. If you want things in your wedding planning, your marriage, and your life to run smooth, communicate, communicate, communicate.

Table #19: Random (But Useful) Tips. Utilize each and every one of these tips given from post-brides, vendors, and others involved in wedding planning. You'll find some gems in here. You can thank me later.

Table #20: The After Party. Of course it's the recap you just read, but it's also the rest of your lives together. I can only hope this book has offered you the unique perspective it offered to me as I wrote it. I also hope it provided some comfort in knowing others have experienced what you have (and will,) and that it's OK. It's your day, so do it your way. And most of all, enjoy!

Works Cited:

Table #3: Bridal Party

The Free Dictionary by Farlex. http://www.thefreedictionary.com/catatonic.

Table #4: In-Laws & Other Family Members

Nicole Yorio. "Should You Go On Wife Strike? – Good Stuff!" Café Mom. July 6, 2011. http://www.cafemom.com/group/111698/forums/read/14439708/Should_You_Go_on_a_Wife_Strike_Good_stuff

Table #5: Haters

Martha Beck. "How to Handle the Narcissists in Your Life." Oprah.com. August 2003. http://www.oprah.com/omagazine/Martha-Beck-Self-Esteem-or-Narcissism

Martha Beck. "How to Get the World to See the Real You: Martha Beck's 4-Step Plan." Oprah.com. October 2010. http://www.oprah.com/spirit/Charisma-and-Self-Confidence-Martha-Becks-Strategy/2

Table #6: Ceremony

Rodgers, Drs. Tom and Beverly. *Soul Healing Love.* Selah Publishing Group, LLC. December 1, 2006. Print.

Culture Ledger. http://www.cultureledger.com/

Environmental Graffiti. http://www.environmentalgraffiti.com/

Infozooms. "10 Extremely Bizarre Wedding Traditions." http://www. infozooms.com/Lists/ListDetails.aspx?rid=149

Marston, Ralph. "Yet You Can."

Table #8: The Dress

Orenstein, Peggy. *Cinderella Ate My Daughter.* Harper. January 25, 2011. Print.

Table #10: Bridal Shower & Big Box Marts

Pink, Daniel. *A Whole New Mind: Why Right-Brainers Will Rule the Future.* Riverhead Trade. March 7, 2006. Print.

Table #12: Your Mental Health

Street-Porter, Janet. *Life's Too F***ing Short:* A Guide to Getting What You Want Out of Life Without Wasting Time, Effort, or Money. Celestial Arts. September 15, 2009. Print.

Table #14: Bling Bling Miss Thing

"It's an Endless Wedding!" *Endless Simmer.* http://www.endlesssimmer.com/2011/08/23/its-an-endless-wedding/

Epstein, Edward J. "Have You Ever Tried to Sell A Diamond?" Atlantic Magazine. February, 1982. http://www.theatlantic.com/magazine/archive/1982/02/have-you-ever-tried-to-sell-a-diamond/304575/

"What Are Blood Diamonds?" Ring Envy. http://www.ringenvy.com/engagement-rings/blood-diamonds

Table #15: Hair, Makeup & Your Inner Fashionista

Rosemarie Pomilla. N.Y. Prostyle Bridal. http://www.nyprostyle.com/bridal/dos-donts

Table #18: Communication

Holmes, Rupert. Lyrics. "Escape." *Partners in Crime.* CD. MCA Records. 1982.

Campion, Caroline. "The Curse of the Just-OK Marriage." Glamour Weddings. http://www.glamour.com/weddings/2011/04/the-curse-of-the-just-ok-marriage

Personal Interviews

Frohboese, Laura. MSW, LCSW

Hardy, Scott R. NC DRC Certified Mediator

Lawson, Laura. MSW, LCSW

Petruk, Leslie. MA, LPC, NCC

Restiano, Ricky. Owner-Operator, Ricky Restiano Photography

Rodgers, Drs. Tom and Beverly

39492005R00151

Made in the USA
Middletown, DE
17 January 2017